BREAKTHROUGH MARKETING PLANS

BREAKTHROUGH MARKETING PLANS

How to Stop Wasting Time and Start Driving Growth

Second Edition

TIM CALKINS

Kellogg School of Management

palgrave
macmillan

BREAKTHROUGH MARKETING PLANS
Copyright © Tim Calkins, 2012.

First published in 2012 by
PALGRAVE MACMILLAN®
in the United States—a division of St. Martin's Press LLC,
175 Fifth Avenue, New York, NY 10010.

Where this book is distributed in the UK, Europe and the rest of the world,
this is by Palgrave Macmillan, a division of Macmillan Publishers Limited,
registered in England, company number 785998, of Houndmills,
Basingstoke, Hampshire RG21 6XS.

Palgrave Macmillan is the global academic imprint of the above companies
and has companies and representatives throughout the world.

Palgrave® and Macmillan® are registered trademarks in the United States, the
United Kingdom, Europe and other countries.

ISBN: 978–0–230–34033–6

Library of Congress Cataloging-in-Publication Data

Calkins, Tim.
    Breakthrough marketing plans : how to stop wasting time and start
    driving growth / Tim Calkins.—2nd ed.
      p. cm.
    ISBN 978–0–230–34033–6 (pbk.)
      1. Marketing—Planning. I. Title.

HF5415.13.C253 2012
658.8′02—dc23   2012022501

A catalogue record of the book is available from the British Library.

Design by Newgen Imaging Systems (P) Ltd., Chennai, India.

First edition: December 2012

10 9 8 7 6 5 4 3 2 1

Printed in the United States of America.

For Carol, Claire, Charlie, and Anna

CONTENTS

Chapter 1

INTRODUCTION

IT WAS NOT A GOOD DAY WHEN Procter & Gamble marketer Kathleen Carroll learned she was being put in charge of Puritan cooking oil. The brand had been struggling for many years, and there was little reason to think things were about to change. Indeed, when her manager briefed her on the business, Kathleen got the distinct impression that her job was mainly to phase out the brand. This was not a career-enhancing assignment.

As Kathleen learned about the Puritan brand, she realized that the situation wasn't hopeless at all. The product was good. It had a point of difference in the market that people cared about; it had a unique blend of sunflower and safflower oils that many believed provided important health benefits. As she recalled, "Everything about it was perfect. The target was just off."[1]

So Kathleen put together a marketing plan to rejuvenate the brand through a bold repositioning. The plan involved three key initiatives: introduce a new product formula, communicate its health benefits, and reach food editors. Kathleen presented the plan to the division president and received approval to move forward. She explained, "I sold them on the fact that the brand could be relaunched."[2]

The results were striking. Kathleen and her cross-functional team executed the plan, and the business responded, with share more than doubling over the next three years.

*   *   *

The ability to craft a strong marketing plan is a critical skill. Business leaders who can create a thoughtful, strategic, and focused plan can have a huge impact on an organization. Plans are vitally important.

I have been writing and reviewing marketing plans for more than twenty years, and teaching people how to write good marketing plans for more than a decade. During this time, I've reviewed more than 3,000 marketing plans from organizations all around the world. This book reflects what I have learned during that time.

Breakthrough Marketing Plans is built upon three very simple propositions. First, marketing plans are important for every organization and every marketer. Indeed, it is virtually impossible to be a successful marketing leader today if you can't create a clear, effective plan and then gain support for it from senior management and your cross-functional team.

Second, a startling number of marketing plans written today are completely ineffective. Many should simply be put in the trash—or, better yet (from an environmental perspective), the recycling bin. Despite the fact that people and organizations frequently spend months working on a marketing plan, the final document often contributes little. All too many marketing plans are reviewed in a perfunctory way and then put on a shelf, where they function as highly effective dust-gathering devices. This wastes time and money, and considering the power of a good marketing plan, it is a missed opportunity.

Third, creating a good marketing plan is really not all that complicated; the theories behind accomplishing this task reflect a good deal of common sense. Indeed, the very best marketing plans are strikingly simple. They are short and easy to understand.

I suspect that after reading this book you might say to yourself, "Well, that seems pretty obvious." And you would be correct; the basic principles behind creating a good marketing plan are not complex. Yet many marketing plans do not follow these basic principles; far too many plans fall victim to the problems described in this book. As one of my students wrote on a class evaluation form, "The strategies discussed were very intuitive and based on common sense. The fact that I could not come up with any of the strategies on my own further showed that common sense, after all, is not very common."

This book has two goals. The first is to highlight the fact that many marketing plans are ineffective and there is an urgent need for change. The second is to help people create stronger marketing plans that galvanize an organization and deliver strong business results.

WHO NEEDS THIS BOOK?

This book is for people who create or review marketing plans. This includes people in large and small organizations, people in for-profit and not-for-profit organizations, and people in new and old companies. This includes those who work in marketing, of course, but also people who perform other functions. Indeed, anyone who writes or reviews a marketing plan can benefit from reading this book.

Breakthrough Marketing Plans is primarily for people new to writing marketing plans, such as business school students and people transitioning into marketing from other functions. To these individuals, this book is an introduction to marketing plans and a guide to what to do and what not to do when creating them.

This book is also valuable for more seasoned marketers, people familiar with the marketing planning process. For these people, *Breakthrough Marketing Plans* has a slightly different purpose: to highlight how marketing plans go awry and to help improve them. After reading this book, some people will want to completely rethink how they approach marketing plans and adopt the ideas here.

Finally, this book is for senior executives, the people accountable for leading an organization and delivering results. Senior managers are, at the end of the day, the people who approve marketing plans and the people who are most accountable for the results. These are also some of the people who are most frustrated by the plans currently being written. Some senior executives may want to use the ideas in this book to improve the marketing plans being written in their organization. Others may use the book to create a formal marketing planning process if one doesn't already exist.

Not everyone will agree with the ideas in this book. People wedded to the traditional marketing plan format, for example, may well reject the ideas presented here; this book is a call for change, and many people don't like change. For those willing to look at things in a fresh way, read on.

USING THIS BOOK

If you are working on a marketing plan that is due in the relatively near future, flip directly to chapter 10. This chapter provides a template for a marketing plan; if time is short, simply follow the template provided. You will find the template a pretty good starting point; it will certainly get you moving in the right direction.

If you don't know whether or not you should be worrying about marketing plans in the first place, start with chapter 2, which explains why every organization needs one.

If you have a bit more time, you can immerse yourself fully in the topic and the theories. Chapter 3 describes the typical marketing plan and highlights why it frequently misses the mark. This chapter also explores the factors that lead to weak plans and examines this rather important question: Why do smart, experienced people create terrible marketing plans? Chapter 4 reviews the key elements of a marketing plan. Chapter 5 describes the characteristics of the best plans.

Chapter 6 presents a planning process with a step-by-step approach. If you are just starting to develop a plan, this will be particularly useful. Chapter 7 includes advice about and suggestions for actually writing the document. Chapter 8 provides best practices for presenting a marketing plan effectively.

Chapters 9 to 13 provide tools and answer questions. Chapter 9 presents twenty strategic initiatives to highlight the range of options available and spark your thinking. Chapter 10 presents a marketing plan template. Chapter 11 reviews frequently asked questions. The book finishes with two marketing plan examples. Chapter 12, a plan in a presentation format, is for Flahavan's, a brand of Irish oatmeal. Chapter 13 is a written plan for Edzo's Burger Shop, a restaurant in Evanston, Illinois.

*   *   *

Creating a strong marketing plan is a critical job for marketers. Unfortunately, far too many people do a miserable job of it. The ideas in this book can help marketers create plans that are approved and supported and that drive strong results. The ideas may also encourage more than a few people to deposit their current marketing plans in the recycling bin and start over.

Chapter 2

WHY BOTHER?

IF YOU CAN CREATE, SECURE SUPPORT FOR, and execute a strong marketing plan, you can have a huge impact on a business. If you can't, you will struggle.

Hewlett-Packard CEO Léo Apotheker provides a rather notable example of this. On August 18, 2011, Apotheker revealed his plan for growing the company. It included the acquisition of a software company, Autonomy, and the likely spin-off of the Personal Systems Group. He positioned the moves as critical for the long-term health of HP, saying, "We are at a pivotal part of our history."[1]

The impact was almost immediate; HP shares plunged as skeptical investors sold their holdings. The stock dropped from a price of $29.51 per share just before the announcement to $23.60 per share. Analysts questioned the strategy, wondering how it could be successful.

Apotheker tried desperately to convince people that his plan made sense, but he failed to do so. HP's board fired him on September 22. As Chairman Ray Lane explained the decision at the time, "We are at a critical moment and we need renewed leadership to successfully implement our strategy and take advantage of the market opportunities ahead."[2]

*   *   *

Marketing plans set the course; the plan spells out the goals for the business over a certain period of time and what precisely should be done to achieve those goals.

More than anything, marketing plans are recommendations; a marketing plan states precisely what steps should be taken to drive the business forward. As Sharon D'Agostino, president of Johnson & Johnson's Consumer Products Division, observed about marketing plans, "This is where we're going, and this is how we're getting there."

A marketing plan is the point of connection between data and action. It is the place where an executive takes all the information available and turns it into a plan for the business.

In many respects, a marketing plan is the focal point. It is where a marketing leader boils down everything she knows about a business and identifies the most important initiatives. Those initiatives are then broken out into all the various tactics and activities (see Exhibit 2.1).

Ultimately, marketing adds value when it leads to action, because action leads to results. In most companies, profits matter most. When profit results are good, everything works at the organization: bonuses are generous, stock options can grow dramatically in value, promotions come along more frequently, and people are fundamentally happy. The reverse is also true: when profit results are bad, bonuses are lower, the value of the stock options falls, employees are under pressure, and people are grumpy. Having experienced both scenarios

Exhibit 2.1   Role of a Marketing Plan

firsthand, I can say for certain that it is far more enjoyable to work at a business when results are good.

Marketing contributes to an organization when it leads to action, and *only* then. Knowing a lot about your consumer is a lovely thing, but all that knowledge will add no value if it isn't put into action. Having insights into what motivates consumers is interesting and important, but the only way it will have an impact on the business is if those insights are turned into recommendations.

Marketing doesn't work unless something actually happens: an advertising campaign goes on television, a new product hits the market, or a price changes. One reason the marketing department is sometimes accused of being out of touch with the business is that marketers sometimes focus on insights and never get around to actually doing anything.

While writing this book, I spoke with dozens of marketing executives who have reviewed and created marketing plans. The most common analogy I heard in those interviews was this: A marketing plan is a road map for a business. The words were almost always the same:

> "It is a road map for where you are going."
> "It's the road map for the future."
> "The marketing plan is the road map."
> "The reason you do the plan is to lay out the road map."

In any business, it is important to remember that a marketing plan is a set of directions. It is a description of what needs to be done to get from one place to another: turn left here, turn right here, go fifty-seven miles, turn left, and you are there.

EVERY ORGANIZATION NEEDS A PLAN

In 2003, the American Dental Association launched what it called the Institute for Diversity in Leadership. This program was established to build the leadership capabilities of dentists from traditionally under-represented groups. During the program, participants created and led public service projects. As a faculty member for the program, I had the opportunity to listen to the very impressive project updates.

One dentist had led a noble program to provide dental services to homeless veterans in San Francisco. The program provided an exceptionally important and valuable service in a very efficient manner. There was one problem, however: the program needed more dentists to volunteer. Otherwise, it would be impossible for the program to grow, impossible for it to reach its full potential, and impossible for it to have a meaningful impact on the pressing human need.

I asked the project leader some basic questions: "So what are you doing to attract more dentists? How are you going to market the opportunity? What is your marketing plan?"

This led to an awkward silence. The dentist shuffled around a bit and looked this way and that. He then rather sheepishly admitted that he had given no thought to marketing the opportunity. "I'm no marketer. I'm just a clinician," he finally said.

He knew, and I knew, that although he was indeed a clinician, he was also a marketer. He marketed his dental practice every day, and in this particular case, he needed to market his volunteer opportunity.

Marketing is the process of connecting products, services, and ideas to customer needs. It is essential for every organization; if you can't link your product or service or idea to a customer need, you will not be successful. People don't buy things for no reason. People spend money, energy, and time on things that they need or want. In other words, people buy things that provide a benefit to them.

This applies to everything; it's hard to imagine something that isn't affected by marketing to some degree. Consumer products are, of course, dependent on marketing. People buy toothpaste to prevent cavities, have healthy gums, or whiten their teeth. Companies engage consulting firms to provide insights and recommendations and ultimately to improve results and increase profits. Restaurants depend on marketing. Retailers, banks, cleaners, and circuses depend on marketing. So do politicians, religious leaders, and environmentalists. They all need people to believe there is a reason to support them; there has to be a benefit.

Each year the industry magazine *Advertising Age* publishes a list of fifty notable marketers: "Fifty Sharp Ideas and the Visionaries Who Saw Them Through." The list is always fascinating because these individuals, who are leaders in innovative marketing efforts, come from a wide range of industries: consumer packaged goods, automotive, health, nonprofit, and financial services, among others. The 2007 list, for example, included the usual suspects, such as Coke and Vaseline, and some more unexpected products and brands, such as the book *The 4-Hour Workweek*; a new commercial airplane, the Boeing 787 Dreamliner; a computer game, *Guitar Hero II*; and a thong, Hanky Panky (see exhibit 2.2).[3]

We are all marketers. As William Luther wrote in his book *The Marketing Plan*, "The central ideas of marketing are universal and it makes no difference whether we are marketing furnaces, insurance policies, or margarine."[4]

Marketing is essential for all companies; every organization has to make choices about what to do and what not to do when it comes to reaching customers. As a result, marketing plans provide an opportunity for every business organization. Marketer Greg Wozniak has seen the broad relevance of marketing plans. He began his career at Kraft Foods, one of the largest food companies in the world. He then moved to Barilla Pasta, a much smaller and privately held company. Later still he started his own company, selling doors to residential building contractors. At each organization, Greg created and used marketing plans, whether he was managing hundred-million-dollar brands at Kraft or launching his small door company. The plans were different in scope and size, but the basic function was the same: to set the course for the business. As he observed, "Marketing plans are applicable to any business."

Exhibit 2.2   2007 *Advertising Age* 50 Notable Marketers

Activia	Alli
Always	Caribou Coffee
Chipotle	Chocolate
Claritin-D	Coke Zero
CPK frozen pizza	Crest Pro-Health
CR-V	Doritos
Dreamliner	Energizer
Facebook	*The 4-Hour Workweek*
Guitar Hero II	*Halo 3*
Hanky Panky	Havaianas
Heineken Premium Light	HP computers
iPhone	JCPenney
Jenny Craig	Johnnie Walker Blue
Keen	Laura's Lean Beef
Life Is Good	Moosejaw
Mucinex	Ray-Ban
7-Eleven	Seventh Generation
SIGG	Skinny Bitch's
Smart Balance	Soleil
Sparks	Special Dark
SpudWare	Stride
SweetLeaf Stevia	Tresemmé
Umpqua	Vaseline
Webkinz	Wrangler Unlimited
Yahoo Answers	Yelp

THE CHALLENGE

Marketing plans are becoming more important because the world is getting more complicated.

Marketing has never been a simple endeavor. It has never been easy to understand what consumers actually want; people may say one thing but want something else, or they may not be able to envision the future or even conceive of what is possible. It has never been easy to deal with competition; competitors have been battling it out for market share for centuries. It has never been easy to create powerful communication; this was true in the Middle Ages, and it is still true today.

Nonetheless, marketing is getting harder. Two factors are driving this change.

TOO MUCH DATA

The first factor making life difficult for marketers is data; quite simply, there is too much information. Marketers today have access to more data than ever before. On some businesses, you can look at sales data by hour, by store, and by product. The amount of information available is stunning, and the amount of time one could spend analyzing this information is infinite.

Intel recently published a report illustrating what happens in a single minute on the Internet: 100,000 new tweets on Twitter, 6 million Facebook views, 6 new Wikipedia articles, 47,000 app downloads, and 30 hours of new videos.[5]

Every day, market research firm Nielsen records 51.5 million transactions at 36,000 stores and sales of 2.1 million books at 12,000 locations. It also tracks 40,000 television programs and 300,000 radio ads.[6]

And the problem is only getting worse. The market research industry, for example, is identifying more and more ways to understand customers. A marketer can conduct focus groups, run quantitative studies, carry out ethnographies, look at brain scans, do conjoint analyses, and conduct elaborate multivariate regression analyses. Interesting new research techniques are appearing all the time, each one creating more data and more information. With the rise of the Internet and the decrease of computing costs, it is possible to segment consumers into smaller and smaller groups. The concept of true one-to-one marketing is now close to becoming reality.

The large amount of data available today is a blessing, certainly. Marketers can now make better decisions than ever before; they can dig into information and uncover remarkable insights and then use these insights to create compelling programs. Several years ago, marketers would never have dreamed of having so much information.

But the vast amount of data is also a curse. If a marketer isn't careful, she will simply get lost in the data. She will spend so much time gathering and analyzing the data that she will never get around to drawing conclusions and answering the most basic questions: So what? What does all this mean? What will we do? As Walmart CMO Stephen Quinn observes, "We have so much data we are drowning in it."

When everything can be analyzed, it gets harder to reach a conclusion. Analysis is easy. Making a decision is hard.

The problem is that the data doesn't really matter. Having lots of facts and figures doesn't necessarily lead to good results. It is just information. What matters is the recommendation: Based on everything we know, what should we do?

AN EXPLOSION OF CHOICE

The second factor making life difficult is the explosion of choice; marketers now have more options than ever before.

Making decisions has always been the hard part of marketing. Ultimately, a marketer has to decide what steps to take to drive sales and build the business. Marketing is all about making choices; a company can't do everything. Ultimately, an organization has to decide how to best utilize scarce resources: time, money, attention, and so forth. This is difficult because marketers could do hundreds or even thousands of things to sell a product.

The list is only getting longer as technology advances; each day, it seems, another compelling marketing tactic arrives in the market, another wonderful thing to pursue. Andy England, global CMO of MillerCoors, appreciates the challenge, noting, "There used to be three choices. Now there are a thousand."

Pretend for a moment that you are the brand manager for Heinz ketchup. What are all the things you could do to drive sales and build profits in the United States? The list is long. You could advertise on network television, on one of the four big networks. Or you could advertise on cable television, on one of dozens of channels. You could advertise in one of the hundreds of magazines on the market, or in one of the hundreds of newspapers. You could increase or decrease prices or run a promotion. If you are running a promotion, you could run it nationally or just in a particular area, and you could run the promotion continuously for a year or pick just one of the fifty-two different weeks. You could improve the product so it performs better or you could reduce its cost. You could change the label or the package. You could create a new flavor. You could launch an entirely new brand or create a sub-brand. You could sponsor the Olympics or a local sporting event. You could do a program on Facebook or build a website. You could run banner ads on one of millions of different websites. The list goes on and on.

The question isn't which ideas are good ones; many of the ideas would likely work to some degree. Nor is the question which ideas will have immediate impact on the business; many of them would probably do this. Of course, some of the best ideas might not; they might be more long-term focused. The most important question is this: Which ideas are the best ones to build the business?

The only certain thing if you are running Heinz ketchup is that you can't pursue all the ideas; trying to do everything will guarantee failure. There isn't enough money to do everything, even on a relatively big brand like Heinz. Doing more and more things means that each one gets less attention and each one probably is executed less well. You have to choose.

A marketing plan help to address both of these challenges; it first helps marketers boil down the data to determine what is important, and then it helps marketers make decisions.

"If you don't know where you are going," the old expression goes, "any road will get you there." This statement is true in life, and it is true in marketing; if you don't know what you are trying to accomplish, everything might be a good idea, and it is impossible to decide.

Without a plan, it is very hard to make decisions about programs. If there is no clear strategy, every program must be considered on tactical merits; it is impossible to determine what is "on strategy" and what is "off strategy." By default, decisions are then made based on short-term benefits. The result is slow decision making and a lack of synergy across the company, or, as one marketing consultant observed about a client, "It's very haphazard. There is no real logic to how they are going to market."

With a clear marketing plan, however, decisions are easier; a marketer can quickly assess options and rule out those that don't fit the plan. As Unilever marketer Andrew Gross said, "If the strategy is clear, then you can tell if an idea fits the strategy."

ALIGNING THE ORGANIZATION

One way marketing plans add value is by creating organizational alignment: getting everyone on the same page and working together. As marketer Dawn Pickett Leijon observed, "It provides the glue for a lot of moving pieces."[7]

Integration is fast becoming a "must do" in the world of marketing; different programs need to work together to maximize the total impact on the business.

This makes sense; tactics should be coordinated and synergistic so that together the efforts accomplish a mission. The television spots for a brand shouldn't be completely different from the print ads, and the sales brochures shouldn't be completely different from the website.

Integration matters for two reasons. First, it can increase the impact of a campaign, so its total is greater than the sum of its parts. The theory is that a customer who sees a television ad, and then an online spot, and then a promotion is more likely to grasp the campaign than someone who sees only the promotion or just two television ads.

Second, integration is important for building a strong brand. Brands are the associations linked to a service or product, and the best brands are clearly defined. A strong brand needs consistent communication to create clear associations in the market.

Great television advertising is a good thing, of course, but in the absence of an integrated plan, it will fall short of its potential. A bold pricing move might be a terrific idea, but if it doesn't fit into a broader plan for a business, it will not work; promotion and sales efforts must support the price move, and the business has to be able to meet changes in demand. A brilliant new product will only succeed if the plan to launch it makes sense.

Toyota presents a wonderful recent example of integration. The company leveraged multiple marketing tactics in 2007 to support the launch of its new Toyota Tundra full-size pickup truck. Toyota used television ads on network and cable stations, print ads, online advertising, a website, local events, sales brochures, dealer events, and giveaway items to support the launch. All the elements worked together because they communicated the same thing and utilized a consistent creative look. Each tactic was different, but the overall feel was the same, giving the campaign far greater impact than if it had been fragmented. All the efforts focused on one goal: building awareness and encouraging key consumers to try out the new Tundra.

A marketing plan plays a key role in driving integration because it keeps all the marketing efforts together in one place. All too often, tactics are developed in isolation; the promotion is developed by the promotion agency, the advertising is created by the advertising agency, and the sales meeting is planned and run primarily by the sales team. The risk, then, is that each program will exist only on its own and lose the sense of integration needed to secure customers.

In a marketing plan, however, the focus is on the total business: what is the overall plan? Once that is known, integrating the tactics is easier because there is a common understanding of the goals and approach. Phil Marineau, former CEO of Levi Strauss, appreciates the importance of a clear plan, noting, "Through leadership and robust planning, you can be very aligned."[8]

It is possible to integrate marketing efforts without a strong marketing plan, but it is much harder to do.

GAINING SUPPORT

At one point in my marketing career, I was put in charge of a legendary brand with very high awareness and a long history. The only problem was that the brand had lost its way in the market; sales had slowly and steadily declined for more than a decade. To prop up profits while sales slumped, my predecessors had cut virtually all the marketing spending and put through cost-reduction projects that saved money, but at the expense of quality.

Concerned by the long-term trend, I worked with my team to put together a plan to rebuild the business by investing in innovation and marketing, improving product quality, and reaching out to attract a new group of consumers. It was a bold plan with a very real chance of reversing the long-term business decline.

The problem, of course, was that the plan was costly. The investments were for the future; improving quality and investing in the brand would yield long-term benefits, but it would take time to see the impact in incremental sales. As a result, profits would decline in the short run.

Before moving ahead with the plan, I needed support from senior management in the company to make the short-term investment. Although the plan was exciting, its costs were real and the investments not insignificant. The challenge for me was clear: Lay out the plan in a way the senior management team would support.

Without senior management support, the plan couldn't move forward. I could create the plan, but I couldn't put it into place.

This is the case in virtually every situation when significant money is in play; nothing happens without support. Before you make big moves, you need approval from senior management. Any time major dollars are at stake, senior people want and need to weigh in. As Harvard professor John Kotter notes, "Well, it's one thing to be able to generate ideas by digging up data, analyzing it, and putting it together in some kind of logical way. But gaining the support you need is an entirely different story."[9]

People need support at every level. A marketing assistant can't roll out a new package design without the approval of the brand manager. A category director can't approve a new product launch without the approval of the division manager. A CEO can't move forward with a dramatic strategic shift without the nod from the board of directors and key investors. As Michael Porter, Jay Lorsch, and Nitin Nohria wrote in a recent *Harvard Business Review* article, "A key CEO role is to sell the strategy and shape how analysts and shareholders look at the company. CEOs should not expect that their strategies will be immediately understood or accepted; a constant stream of reiterations, explanations, and reminders will likely be necessary to affect analysts' perceptions."[10]

People also need support from across the organization. Many companies these days are matrix organizations, where people work together with dotted-line relationships. In this type of environment, gaining support for a plan from key functions is essential. An innovation program will fail without the support of the R&D group. An in-store promotion idea will flop if the sales team doesn't agree. A cost-reduction program will not materialize if the operations group doesn't believe it is possible.

Indeed, the only type of organization for which you can do things without approval is a sole proprietorship; in that type of company, you as the owner just have to convince yourself that you have a good plan, usually an easy task.

A marketing plan is a key vehicle for gaining support; it is the tool managers use to present and gain support for the business. A marketing plan can drive consensus across the organization and serve as a communications vehicle. As marketer Mike Puican said about marketing plans, "The ultimate purpose is to gain agreement."

People must believe in the plan. Setting the course and then communicating and building support for it are core tasks of leadership.

People need to understand where the business is heading so that they have confidence in it and know how their actions contribute to the larger enterprise. General Electric's Jack Welch observed that communicating the direction of a business is a core task of leadership. According to Welch, "People must have the self-confidence to be clear, precise, to be sure that every person in their organization—highest to lowest—understands what the business is trying to achieve."[11] Ford CEO Alan Mulally echoed the point, noting, "I know how successful it can be when a business has a plan, everybody knows the plan, and everybody knows how we are performing against that plan."[12]

This is one of the reasons marketing plans are so important. As Mark Delman, a marketing executive at Adobe, said, "You need a way to communicate to an organization what you are doing." AspireUp's Roland Jacobs agreed, saying, "A good plan serves as a communications piece."

In my case, I used the marketing plan to successfully secure support from senior management and cross-functional leaders for restaging the business. Short-term profit results were poor due to the big investments in improving product quality and strengthening the brand. Eventually, however, profit bounced back as the business improved.

IS IT WORTH IT?

Creating a marketing plan is a choice. It is not like paying taxes, or assembling required financial statements, or paying invoices. An organization can decide to create a marketing plan or not. It is very possible to market a product without a marketing plan. You could simply create a new ad campaign, launch a new product, or roll out a promotion.

So is it really worth the time and effort required to create and write down a marketing plan?

The answer is a resounding yes. Creating a marketing plan almost certainly will produce better results because the very process of writing a plan forces clarity. It is easy to say, "Oh, we'll do this and that," but it's much harder to write down precisely what needs to happen and why it will work.

More important, a clear, focused marketing plan will drive consensus; it can secure key resources and ensure that all cross-functional team members are aligned. For a leader, this is invaluable. A. G. Lafley was CEO of Procter & Gamble from 2000 to 2009. He observed, "Strategic clarity frees up and focuses the entire organization. It reduces complexity and confusion. It enables more consistent, more disciplined, more predictably excellent execution. Consequently, strategic clarity leads to more reliable and sustainable business and financial results."[13]

Spending time creating a plan is an investment that will deliver strong returns.

BE CAREFUL

Writing a very strong marketing plan increases the odds that it will be approved. In a sense, this means you will have the opportunity to try your ideas. As one marketing executive pointed out, "A great plan gives top management confidence in you." Another observed, "You're earning your autonomy with really good plans."

A good plan does not guarantee success; it may increase your odds, but it offers no certainty. You have to be somewhat careful. The better you become at creating strong marketing plans, the more likely it is you will be given the opportunity to implement the plan. As the old saying goes, "Be careful what you wish for."

A person gifted at creating strong plans can take a set of mediocre ideas and get approval. But even if the plan itself wins approval, the bottom-line results are likely to be, well, mediocre.

A good marketing plan gets you to the plate. It gives you the chance to succeed. And because you can't hit a home run from the dugout, getting to the plate is an essential task. Just don't assume that you'll hit a home run every time you get there.

* * *

Every organization in the world needs marketing, and every organization needs a marketing plan. There is so much information and so many marketing tactics that it is almost impossible to make decisions without a plan.

A marketing plan lays out the course for a business, drives integration, and builds support. These are all critical tasks of leadership.

Chapter 3

THE PROBLEMS

"THIS IS AN AWARD-WINNING MARKETING PLAN," the executive gushed as he handed me a thick document. I admired its heft, its beautiful cover page, its perfect binding. I flipped through a few pages; each one was full of information and analysis. "This one received several prizes in the company," the executive continued. "It's a great piece of work."

I thanked him profusely for letting me review the plan, and after unsuccessfully attempting to squeeze the enormous document into my briefcase, I tucked it under my arm and headed back to my office.

Later that day I sat down and started reading the plan. I read about the industry, the competition, and the challenges facing the business. I read about the distributors and suppliers, and about all the different trends playing out in the industry. I read about potential capacity issues and regulatory changes on the horizon. I read about recent results. And, more than anything else, I read about consumers: who buys, why they buy, why they don't buy, their motivations and their desires.

As I read the plan, I quickly realized that the brand faced some significant business issues; profit was well below goal, and even more substantial challenges lay ahead because of tough competitive dynamics. It was a very difficult situation.

Eventually, after many hours, I finally found my way to the second part of the plan, the actual recommendations. This section included a vast array of programs, such as promotions, advertising campaigns, sales contests, public relations campaigns, and pricing changes. All of the programs were laid out in great detail with the cost calculated down to the dollar. Near the end of the plan was a very complete calendar, showing all the activities scheduled for the following year.

It took me several days to get through the entire plan, and when I finally finished reading it, I was overwhelmed. The plan had gone on for 259 pages, single-spaced. The document contained 45,879 words. It was longer than many novels and about the size of this entire book. It was an impressive document, clearly the product of months of work by a knowledgeable and motivated team.

But the more I thought about the plan, the more puzzled I became. The first part of the document had identified some major business challenges. The second part presented all sorts of tactics and programs. But there was no link between the two parts; despite its considerable length, the plan contained no explanation of how the recommended tactics would address the issues. Why would the plan work, anyway? How would all the programs deliver improved results?

I phoned the executive who gave me the plan and asked him about the rather distant connection between the plan's first part (the issues and analysis) and the second part (the tactics). "Well, you know, that's a pretty good question," he conceded. He thought for a minute and then observed, "Of course, you're probably the first person who has actually read the entire plan."

He was right, of course. The marketing plan, although the product of hours and hours of work, had never been read by anyone. This shouldn't have come as a surprise. How many business leaders have time to sit down and read a single-spaced marketing document the size of a textbook? Most executives run from meeting to meeting, checking e-mail as they go. They hardly have time to flip through the *Wall Street Journal*. The thoroughly researched, elegantly produced, and intensely reviewed plan had never been read. Incredibly, the plan—and all the work that went into it—was largely a waste of time. Not surprisingly, the business did poorly, substantially missing its profit target.

Unfortunately, my research and experience suggest that this isn't unusual at all. Although many companies devote an extraordinary amount of time and effort to marketing plans, more often than not the end results are long, complicated documents that say little and frequently aren't even read. As Chicago advertising executive Stuart Baum noted, "In many companies, if you put a five-dollar bill between page 16 and 17 of the marketing plan, no one would ever find it."

The overall situation is rather grim; executives across industries are frustrated with tedious and pointless marketing plans. At best, these irrelevant tomes simply consume time and resources. At worst, they suck energy and creativity from an organization.

The discontent spans companies and industries. Karen David-Chilowicz, a marketing veteran with experience at Prudential and Western Union, thinks most plans don't work very well. She notes, "Maybe 20 percent of companies do it right. Many have absolutely no clue." Michael McGrath, a marketing executive at pharmaceutical giant Eli Lilly, is less optimistic. His opinion: "Five percent of marketing plans are good." Consumer goods marketer and private equity investor Andy Whitman is more direct, declaring simply, "Most of them suck."

This is an enormous problem. For many executives, creating a marketing plan is a time-consuming and frustrating experience, notable mainly for what the process doesn't produce: a clear direction for how a business will build sales and profits. The truth is that many and perhaps most marketing plans are a vast waste of time and money, an unwieldy recitation of facts and details. The marketing plan ends up on a bookshelf, unread.

In many companies, marketing is coming under attack; people are raising tough questions about what marketing actually contributes. One sign of the discontent is the growing chorus of people demanding concrete return on investment (ROI) figures for marketing programs. Another sign is the pace of turnover in the ranks of chief marketing officers (CMOs); a recent study by executive recruiter Spencer Stuart found that the average tenure for a CMO was just 23.6 months, less than half the average tenure for a CEO.[1]

The typical marketing plan does little to dispel the belief that marketing does not contribute significantly to the organization. A marketing plan that is mostly an irrelevant collection of facts and data contributes mightily to the view that marketing itself is largely irrelevant, too. This is an embarrassment for the entire marketing industry.

THE USUAL DOG AND PONY SHOW

If you've worked in marketing for any length of time, you're most likely very familiar with the typical marketing plan; you know the drill all too well.

The marketing plan is a long document, perhaps one or two hundred pages, or even more. It is polished, often a carefully crafted PowerPoint presentation. The pages are colorful, full of graphs and charts. The binding—and it is always bound in some fashion—is perfect. The document is labeled with something authoritative, perhaps: "Electronics Division 2013–2014 Marketing Plan." It is clear that the team spent hours and hours creating the document.

The first—and often biggest—part of the plan is the situation analysis. This section reviews what the team knows about the business and the category. The amount of information it contains is often astounding. There might be a review of the current products, an analysis of key competitors, an overview of trends in the industry, a discussion of product cost issues, and a recap of recent activities and results. In companies with a more external emphasis, a vast amount of information is given regarding customers, ranging from segmentation study results to findings from the latest round of focus groups.

After the situation analysis, the plan moves on to recommendations. These are usually organized around marketing's four Ps (price, promotion, place, and product) or around functions (advertising, promotions, sales, and R&D), or both. Often, each of the sections is written by the functional group that knows it best, so the sales group writes the sales section, the operations group writes the operations section, and the new products team writes the new products section.

The recommendation section of the plan is lengthy; it includes all the scheduled programs for the upcoming year or two. In many cases the detail is extensive. The advertising section, for example, might include a five-page discussion of the media plan alone, including several potential schedules that show possible media-mix combinations. In one version, the media spending might be concentrated on network television. Another version might show a mix of network television, cable television, and radio. Yet another version might feature reduced network television, with more social media programs.

The plan then moves on to a financial section, where budget projections are laid out in detail for the next several years. This might include an analysis of cash flow and capital expenditures, and it will often show margin trends across multiple dimensions.

The typical plan is frequently paired with an exceptionally robust appendix, which includes all the findings and ideas that didn't make it into the situation analysis or the rest of the plan. Indeed, in some cases a page stands ready to address every possible question someone might ask about the business. In one notable example, a team wrote a one-hundred-page marketing plan and then created a two-hundred-page appendix.

After months of development, the marketing team presents this document to senior management. The team reserves the largest available conference room and rehearses extensively in the days leading up to the presentation. The day before the meeting is a scramble as people try to finish the presentation and then run copies. Just making all the needed copies takes much of the day.

On the day of the meeting, the team arrives early to set up the room; its members carefully arrange the chairs and tables, make sure breakfast is ready, and double-check that all the props are at hand.

As the start time approaches, the marketing team settles in, and then the senior executive team arrives. An often substantial number of other interested but tangentially involved people file in too: the lawyers, the human resources team, and the procurement group. Finally, the lights dim and the team launches into the well-polished show. Sixty people, sometimes more, look on with excitement and anticipation. It is a glorious show to which everyone who is anyone in the company wishes to be invited.

Over the course of the next several hours, the excited and nervous business team presents the plan, going through the lengthy presentation page by page. The presenters review the agenda, the situation analysis, and the recommended programs. Various team members stand up to present a few pages and then sit down. The team methodically moves through the slides. Questions, if there are any, are handled smoothly, perhaps with the use of a page from the appendix.

About three hours later, the team wraps things up, right on schedule. The audience smiles and applauds the team's tremendous work and great ideas. The comments are frequently the same: "This is an impressive plan that clearly reflects a tremendous amount of work. Well done!" Or, "It's wonderful to see this kind of analytic and creative thinking about the business. The team deserves a lot of credit for doing such a good job!" Or, "I'm truly impressed with the plan. It won't be an easy year, but I think this plan is a tremendous document." After one or two rather perfunctory questions, everyone heads off. The business team goes out to lunch and takes the afternoon off. And with that, another year's marketing plan passes into history.

A WASTE OF TIME

The problem, of course, is that the entire exercise was essentially a waste of time; the business team invested weeks creating the plan—which then contributed almost nothing.

The plan failed to set a clear course for the business. Although it contained much data and many insights, it had no theme, no overall story people could remember. The overall takeaway was, "Wow, you know a lot and are doing a lot of things." This is neither memorable nor distinctive. It is work for the sake of showing the company you are working.

Most important, the plan failed in its most basic task: it didn't gain agreement on the overall direction for the business. The senior executives who reviewed the plan didn't say anything bad about it, but they didn't necessarily endorse it, either. It wasn't actually given the green light.

This lack of support is a huge problem for the people charged with running the business. Without agreement on the plan, each tactical decision comes up for review, discussion, and scrutiny.

This leads to frustration and unproductive discussions regarding execution. When presenting a new public relations campaign, for example, a team might hear something like this from a senior executive: "So tell me again, what are the goals for this program? How much are we spending? Do we really need to do this?" The questioning of the tactic reflects a lack of understanding of the broader picture. It is also incredibly frustrating for the team managing the project; it sends the members right back to square one.

The lack of agreement also leads to problems when it comes to finalizing financial plans. In many cases, in order to make the financial targets, spending on marketing programs gets reduced, generally without a concurrent reduction in sales targets. Of course, when a marketing plan is just a collection of tactics, it seems easy and painless to reduce spending: "Oh, we can run fewer ads or spend less on the website."

So, despite the weeks the team invested in creating an ornate marketing plan—assembled and bound with such care—it ultimately contributed little to the business.

WHAT WENT WRONG?

Anytime a commercial airplane crashes, investigators study the event to see what went wrong. The emergency responders locate the black box that recorded everything that occurred leading up to the crash, and a team of aviation experts sits down to reconstruct the scene and figure out precisely what happened. More important, the experts try to figure out what can be done to prevent future crashes.

The same process can be applied to marketing plans. Why, precisely, do so many of them end up meaning so little? When plans go awry, what happened? What can be done to prevent future incidents?

During the process of researching this book, I asked dozens of marketing and business executives about marketing plans. In particular, I asked them where plans fall short. When a plan doesn't work, what happened? From my research, I discovered five very common problems or pitfalls.

THE TOP FIVE PROBLEMS

1. Too much data
2. No strategy
3. Lack of rationale
4. Unrealistic thinking
5. No focus

These five problems are almost universal. If a marketing plan is weak, very often one of these five problems lurks behind the picture. Let's take a look at these problems in detail.

1. Too Much Data

The biggest problem in many marketing plans is very simple: the plan includes too much data. It is simply too long and filled with too much information. The plan goes on and on and on.

Many marketing plans are eighty, one hundred, or even two hundred pages long. The plans contain an extraordinary collection of information, virtually everything that is known about the business. Frequently, the marketing plan itself ends up being stuffed with data and then paired with an even longer appendix.

The situation can quickly become absurd. Marketer Kevin McGahren-Clemens spent more than a decade at Kraft Foods before becoming president of American Beverage Corporation. He recalled the moment when he realized the marketing plan process was out of control: "I was on Philadelphia Cream Cheese, and we were going to present the plan. The deck was about 120 or 130 pages, and there were huge filing boxes full of backups. There must have been 1,000 pages. I thought afterwards, look at all the manpower and stress."

One well-known consumer products company embarked on a marketing plan simplification project, putting the emphasis on getting very tight, focused plans. The result of the project was that the average marketing plan at the company dropped from over a hundred pages to about seventy. This was considered a major step forward. Of course, the plan was still far too long; who has time to read seventy pages?

The problem is that all the information hurts rather than helps the plan. It creates several problems. First, the data obscures the most important part of the plan: the actual recommendations. When eighty pages of information and analysis precede it, a set of recommendations will get lost. Many people will never get to the recommendations at all, and those who do will be overwhelmed by the data and complexity.

Second, creating a data-intensive plan is a lengthy process. Simply gathering and formatting the information will take quite a bit of time. As a result, there is a risk that more effort will be spent on laying out the data than on generating or supporting the actual recommendations. As one marketing executive explained, "So much time is spent trying to gather relevant information that the marketer runs out of time to analyze it and determine the implications for the plan. There is too much data and too little analysis and implication."

Some people argue that it is better to include more information than less; if nothing else, a large document suggests that the team has been diligent and worked hard. This line of thinking is fundamentally flawed; unnecessary information clutters the plan and obscures the recommendations. If the information is not directly relevant to the matter at hand, it should not be in the plan. As Mark Shapiro, CEO of Gladson Interactive and a former general manager at Quaker Oats, lamented, "So many presentations are simply one chart after another."

Marketing plans can become bogged down in two places. The first is the situation analysis; this part of the marketing plan all too often goes on and on with no real point. In an effort to present a rigorous situation analysis, the team includes all sorts of information: a list of products, a review of pricing, a deep competitive analysis, an update on new products. Most of it is not needed. Many times, the situation analysis seems like a code for, "Here is all the data we have on this business." As one executive observed, "The temptation is to include every morsel of information gleaned in the market assessment—to the detriment of the plan."

The problem today is simply that far too much information is available regarding any particular business. Just laying out the basics of a business—the important trends, the competitive situation, and the recent performance—can take eighty or ninety pages. But in reality, these eighty or ninety pages accomplish virtually nothing; the information does not lead directly to a recommendation. One plan I reviewed featured a page with a picture of the brand's four products, ignoring the fact that anyone reviewing the plan would almost certainly already know the existing products. Another plan featured a map of the United States showing the breakout of sales by region. Was the regional sales information particularly important? No. It was simply an attractive and totally irrelevant chart. Most marketing plans would improve substantially if the authors dropped the situation analysis and began with the recommendations.

Microsoft's guide to creating a marketing plan provides very clear directions for the situation analysis: "Describe what's happening in the industry and marketing without drawing any conclusion about strategy." This is a recipe for disaster.

The second place where plans can bog down is in the tactics. Many marketing plans include very specific and detailed information on each specific program. The plan includes details on each promotional event, sales contest, and public relations initiative. This is all unnecessary.

A good marketing plan should focus on the key initiatives, not the tactics. Indeed, until there is agreement on the big initiatives, there is no point working through all the tactical details. Finalizing the creative for a coupon supporting a new product, for example, doesn't make any sense until it is certain the new product will be launching and supported by the coupon.

The presentation of detailed tactics quickly shifts the focus of the discussion from big strategy questions to small executional questions. This doesn't help anyone. As one marketing executive observed, if you present too many tactics, "suddenly your presentation to management is all about whether the coupon is 25 cents or 50 cents."

The tactical details should be worked out by the business team and should not be presented to or reviewed by senior executives. As AspireUp's Roland Jacobs said, "Senior management is looking to get results. They don't care about a coupon plan." Reviewing detailed program information with senior management suggests that the team isn't confident in its ability to execute the plan, and it encourages senior people to get involved in minor issues.

The only reason a senior executive needs to review a small tactical decision is if he doesn't trust the team running the business—which is symptomatic of a much bigger problem.

2. No Strategy

A good marketing plan should emphasize strategy. What are we going to focus on to build the business? Strategies should be the heart of the concept, the framework around which the entire plan is built. Unfortunately, many marketing plans fall short when it comes to the strategy.

Several specific problems are to blame. The first is a complete lack of a strategy: the plan jumps directly from the situation analysis to the tactics, skipping the strategy entirely. The plan might present a recommendation for Twitter, for example, before there is agreement about what the business is hoping to do overall.

A marketing plan I recently reviewed from one of the world's largest auto companies provided a perfect example of this problem. The plan started with a review of the situation, including an analysis of the competition and trends in the market. It then jumped directly to tactics: pricing moves, promotion plans, and dealer management. Missing, of course, was the heart of the plan: the strategy.

Another common problem is vague or imprecise phrasing, which results in strategies so broad and general that they are essentially meaningless. One plan I read recently, for example, listed one of the strategies as "pricing." This is an empty strategy; it doesn't provide any direction for the business. What about pricing? Another strategy in the same plan was "innovation." What about innovation? The strategy says nothing.

3. Lack of Rationale

A good marketing plan needs to be persuasive. Someone reading a good marketing plan will understand what the plan is and why it will work. Many plans, however, fail to offer appropriate support for the recommendation. The plan might explain *what* without explaining *why*.

Because one of the most important reasons to create a marketing plan is to gain support across the organization, a marketing plan needs to have a solid rationale.

One fifty-page marketing plan I recently read had twenty pages of recommendations. However, the plan completely lacked any support for the recommendations.

Marketing is really about selling; a marketer spends her time looking for ways to sell a product or service or idea. So it is somewhat surprising how often marketers neglect to sell the marketing plan.

Of course, the structure of many marketing plans makes it hard to provide the needed support. For example, the traditional plan, featuring a thorough situation analysis followed by a series of recommendations, leaves little room for rationale; all the data was presented before any recommendations were made. Connecting the data to the recommendations is left to the reader. This is not the ideal approach.

A good marketing plan provides clear, unambiguous data supporting the recommendations. If the plan is recommending an increase in advertising, the rationale for the spending increase should be clear. If the plan is recommending a public relations effort, the thinking behind the recommendation should be apparent.

4. Unrealistic Thinking

Many marketing plans fail because they are based on wishful thinking; the plan is so optimistic that it is not at all credible.

Wishful thinking can pop up all throughout a plan, from the impact of new products, to the power of different marketing ideas, to the receptivity of distribution partners, to a new program.

Optimism is one of the great downfalls of many business executives, and marketers are perhaps more susceptible than most to its siren call. It is pleasant to assume that things will play out as desired: the new product will succeed, competitors will retreat, and customers will eagerly welcome a price increase. Ignoring the reality of a situation, however, is a certain recipe for trouble. New products generally fail, competitors will almost always complicate your life, and customers will push back against a price increase. Great plans anticipate and incorporate the reality of the situation.

A marketing plan based on optimistic assumptions causes all sorts of problems. First, the plan is rarely credible, so it doesn't get support. Second, the plan rarely works; it doesn't deliver the planned results because things never turn out perfectly. Third, the plan isn't optimal; a more realistic view of the situation would have led to more realistic strategies.

A good marketing plan is based on a realistic view of the situation, the competition, and the capabilities of the company. Assuming that everything will work out fine is both delusional and destructive.

As one seasoned marketer observed, "You need to look reality in the eye."

Stephen Cunliffe, president of Nestlé's frozen foods division, commented that a weak plan is "usually disconnected from reality," noting that many plans are full of optimistic projects and lack any substantive analysis of the competition.

And he's right. A marketing plan must be grounded in the situation as it exists today, not as someone might wish it would be.

5. No Focus

Perhaps the most common problem of all is a general lack of focus. The plan includes so many strategies and tactics that it lacks focus. The ideas might all be good, but there are simply too many of them.

Many marketing plans have eight or nine or even eleven strategies. This is simply too much. I recently flew to Warsaw on LOT Polish Airlines and learned from the in-flight magazine that the airline had twenty-one "must-win battle strategies." That is a lot to keep track of. The U.S. Army developed a marketing plan several years ago that included a remarkable seven priorities, thirteen goals, and thirty-two strategies. The Latin School of Chicago, a prestigious private high school, has a plan with nineteen goals and 105 strategies.[2] How can you focus on 105 things?

Tektronix, a manufacturer of testing equipment, had a plan with 102 strategic objectives and 4,000 tactics. When Martyn Etherington became CMO, he was horrified to learn this. He explained that he found "just a plethora of activities, but not quantifiable metrics or any way that I could quantify that my function was actually making a difference to the business."[3]

Developing strategy is the process of focusing; strategic decision making is all about just that: making decisions. In many ways, an organization that has fifteen strategies has none; without prioritization, there can be no true decision making. A list of fifteen strategies is not actually a list of strategies; it is just a list.

Sergio Pereira, head of marketing at Quill, an office products retailer, noted that having too many strategies is a common problem in marketing plans. He observed, "People always bite off more than they can chew." Adobe's Mark Delman agreed: "It's often five objectives and twenty-five strategies," he said. "The organization just can't handle that."

WHY GOOD PEOPLE CREATE BAD PLANS

Most people who succeed in marketing are smart, strategic thinkers. Marketing is difficult; it is a major challenge to understand consumers and figure out how to meet their needs while differentiating from the competition and driving profits. So the people who succeed in marketing are generally shrewd business leaders.

Why, then, do smart people create marketing plans that contribute so little? Why do good people create bad plans?

IT IS EASY
The first reason why good people create bad plans is simple: it is easy. It isn't hard to create the traditional long, detailed marketing plan. It takes time and effort, of course, but the process is clear: assemble a long, detailed situation analysis; create highly detailed tactical plans with lots of ideas; and produce a glossy, nicely bound document. Indeed, with time, energy, and a good printer, anyone can produce the typical marketing plan, and one that looks polished and thorough to boot.

It is much harder to create a tight, focused marketing plan. Figuring out the key strategies for a business and explaining why they will yield positive results is hard work, requiring thought and analysis. Creating a tight marketing plan takes decisiveness because making choices is difficult. As P&G's A. G. Lafley observed, "Most human beings and most companies don't like to make choices. And they particularly don't like to make a few choices that they really have to live with. They argue, 'It's much better to have lots of options, right?'"[4]

IT FEELS SAFE
A long, detailed marketing plan gives a feeling of safety. Many managers take comfort in data; with enough data, they can answer any

question. A big deck looks impressive. There is something immensely satisfying about handing out a large presentation; the thunk on the table communicates thoroughness, hard work, and credibility.

I spoke with one marketing executive from Coca-Cola who always strove to create the longest marketing plan in the company; she was "proud about that."

Showing up with a compact, focused marketing plan, in contrast, can be scary, in part because the ideas are clear and apparent. Everything looks simple.

General Electric's Jack Welch appreciated the challenge. "You can't believe how hard it is for people to be simple—how much they fear being simple," he said. "They worry that if they're simple, people will think they are simple-minded. In reality, of course, it's just the reverse. Clear, tough-minded people are the most simple."[5]

IT IS TRADITION

Every organization has ways of operating. Organizational culture runs deep, especially in companies that promote from within. As a result, many processes become deeply entrenched in an organization, and marketing planning is one of them.

In many companies, the marketing plan process is a central part of the annual calendar; it has been done for years, and everyone knows what to expect. People plan their vacations around the process.

This type of environment promotes the temptation to follow the norms and stick with tradition. Doing something different is risky. Showing up with a twenty-page plan when everyone in the company knows that a marketing plan should be 150 pages is just too bold for many people. It is safer and easier to adhere to tradition.

IT TURNS INTO THE BUDGET

People sometimes think of the marketing plan as a budget. This is almost always a problem because the plan then becomes far too financially oriented, and the strategic issues get lost.

Organizations need to develop financial forecasts to anticipate and plan for the business. For example, to understand capital needs, a business needs a detailed set of financial projections. Budgeting, after all, is a core business task. In most companies, budgets are exceptionally detailed and rigorous, as they should be.

Detailed financial forecasts are not marketing plans, however, and these two should not travel together. A marketing plan needs to touch on the financials, certainly, but a marketing plan is not a budget.

Loading too much financial information into a marketing plan creates a simple problem; the numbers overwhelm the strategy. This is especially problematic if your audience is financially inclined. If you present a marketing plan that includes detailed numbers to a financially oriented executive, there is a very real chance that the entire conversation will focus on the numbers. Instead of thinking about how precisely a business will compete and what it should emphasize, the discussion becomes geared to the financial questions, such as margin trends and cost forecasts.

Reviewing numbers is not the reason to create a marketing plan; detailed financial projections should be the result—not the input—of a marketing plan. For example, an advertising budget should be set only when the broader strategy is clear; if there is no strategic need for advertising, then there should not be any spending on it, regardless of last year's effort.

One executive with whom I spoke recalled how his division would create thorough and thoughtful marketing plans for each of the company's key products during the annual planning process. The presentation to the CEO, however, included both marketing plans and the financial budget. As a result, the meeting focused solely on the numbers; the marketing plans were never discussed.

It is tempting to load up a marketing plan with financial information. Numbers are factual and easy to obtain. They are also concrete and tangible and much easier to present than concepts, such as marketing initiatives and tactics that are often ambiguous and hard to define precisely. Presenting financial forecasts, however, is not the purpose of a marketing plan.

As one expert on marketing plans wrote, "Preoccupation with preparing a detailed one-year plan first is typical of those many companies who confuse sales forecasting and budgeting with strategic marketing planning—in our experience the most common mistake of all."[6]

BOOKS RECOMMEND IT

Many guides to writing great plans do not help this situation. Most of them actually make it much worse. Consider, for a moment, one of the leading guides to writing marketing plans. The book is a remarkable 630 pages. The recommended table of contents for a marketing plan goes on for three pages. The guide suggests starting the plan with a marketing audit, and the description of this audit goes on for 154 pages.

Another guide to marketing plans starts off with this dynamic sentence: "The purpose of this book is to assist you in developing a sound and profitable marketing plan by creating a desirable positioning or personality for your business based on your Fact Book, which is an analysis of market economics, competition, customers, and your own business, and then make that personality come alive with the execution of unique-to-your-industry marketing tools."[7] Enough said.

In yet another guide to marketing plans, the author issues a warning: "It is strongly advised, however, that you consult your accountant when considering this section, as the methodology described is quite complex."[8]

Sadly, these misguided recommendations are not unusual. Managers who look for ways to improve marketing planning find little to fall back on. It is not a surprise that people looking for help writing great marketing plans find little appropriate guidance, and in the end they waste much time on plans that will have little impact.

Of course, many existing guides to writing marketing plans were created by academics, people who have a deep familiarity with business theory and a great appreciation for knowledge and learning.

It isn't surprising that their recommendations call for, yes, a focus on knowledge and learning. Missing, however, are the questions facing practicing executives: So, what are we going to do? Why will it work, anyway?

*   *   *

In one of the first commercials ever aired for the Dyson vacuum cleaner, inventor James Dyson explained how most vacuum cleaners suffered from a basic problem. "Ever since the vacuum cleaner was invented, it has had a basic design flaw. Bags, filters.... They all clog with dust and then lose suction. The technology simply doesn't work."

The typical marketing plan also suffers from a basic design flaw: it focuses on the details and not on the big picture. It gets lost in the data and the tactics. As a result, such a plan ends up being a waste of time. It is a wonderful dog and pony show, but it ultimately contributes nothing significant to the business.

Chapter 4

THE KEY ELEMENTS

MARKETING PLANS ARE NOT ALL THAT COMPLICATED. You create one for a specific purpose: to set the course for a business and to ensure that everyone is on the same page. It is a working document; you aren't trying to create a literary masterpiece that will take its place beside *War and Peace*. As marketer Greg Wozniak remarked, "It is almost scary how basic it is."

This chapter explains the three key components of a great marketing plan: goals (or objective), strategic initiatives, and tactics. This is the GOST framework. The chapter then demonstrates how the elements can be summarized on one simple page.

GOALS

A marketing plan should be built to achieve something; it is an action-oriented document. For this reason, it is important to start with goals or objectives; you can't develop a plan until you know what you're trying to do.

The goal, or objective, is what the business is trying to achieve through the marketing plan. A goal is not a value, principle, or theory. It is the desired end result.

Don't be confused by the language; either word will do. Some people draw a distinction between the two, claiming that the goal in the marketing plan is different from the objective. According to Dictionary.com, a goal is "the result or achievement toward which effort is directed." An objective is "something that one's efforts or actions are intended to attain or accomplish."[1] My advice: use the words interchangeably and avoid confusion.

A marketing plan should be built around just one or two objectives. A business that has a dozen goals has no focus and no sense of direction. Prioritization isn't clear, and defining success becomes difficult.

A good objective is quantifiable; it is specific and measurable. Good objectives follow the acronym SMART: they are specific, measurable, achievable, relevant, and time specific. A good objective has to be specific, which simply means that it must be clear. Vague objectives are not helpful. Measurement is essential; it should be easy to track your progress. This is the only way to evaluate success and measure progress. Objectives should be achievable and relevant to the business. And they should be time specific. Without a time element, objectives have no urgency. It is a bit like committing to lose weight without committing to a target date; you can always push the target out into the future and have another doughnut or two today.

THE PRIORITY: PROFIT

Marketing plans should be built around financial objectives, ideally profit; the plan should focus on the money.

The core challenge for anyone running a business is building profits because they ultimately drive a company's stock price; increasing stock price is a key task for any manager in a public company. As Diane Primo, chief marketing officer at retailer CDW, observed, "The first thing is 'how am I going to make money here?'"

Ignoring the profit situation of a business is not wise. Managers who deliver strong profit results are generally rewarded, and often handsomely; they are promoted, given big bonuses, and awarded prizes. Effort is not the primary criterion for success in business. Hardworking managers who fail to hit profit objectives are generally punished; they receive small bonuses, are passed over for promotions, and are overlooked for prizes. Early on in my career at Kraft Foods, the head of the Grocery Products Division, Carl Johnson, took me aside and gave me a bit of advice. He explained, "Tim, good numbers don't guarantee your success, but bad numbers will get you every time." And he was absolutely correct.

A recent global survey of corporate managers highlights the importance of hitting the numbers. The survey examined the importance of different leadership qualities. Among them, the number-one most respected leadership quality was clear: the "ability to bring in the numbers." This attracted 36 percent of respondents from the United States and Canada. Interpersonal skills, such as influencing and coaching, were second, with 15 percent of respondents. Strategic thinking was third with 12 percent. Only 4 percent of respondents thought innovation and creativity were the most important.[2] A marketing plan needs ideas and creativity, but more than anything, it has to be grounded in the numbers.

The best way to be certain that a marketing plan is tied to the numbers is to make sure it includes a clear financial objective. As marketer Karen David-Chilowicz explained, "How do you plan a business if you aren't looking at the money coming in and the money going out?" Dell Computer CEO Kevin Rollins observed, "You're in trouble if you don't understand the P&L."[3]

It is almost impossible to create a great marketing plan without a financial objective. Without the full picture, the strategic initiatives and tactics don't tie to the overall financials, and without a link to the financials, the recommendations lose their impact.

Ignoring the financial side of a business is a very good way for a marketer to get into trouble. Without that direct link to the numbers, marketing efforts seem secondary in importance, and other things matter more. For example, if marketing efforts are not tied to the P&L, it's easy to cut the spending; without a link, cutting the marketing budget feels like it will not impact the financial results. Similarly, delaying a key marketing initiative will appear to have no financial ramifications.

This makes marketing vulnerable. As one marketer said, "This, in my opinion, is the key missing element to many marketing plans. How does it tie to the financials?"

One reason many companies today question the effectiveness of marketing is that marketing's role in driving the P&L is not clear. As a result, marketing programs are discussed in isolation, and this makes them seem optional and discretionary.

In the rare circumstance where profit is hard to nail down, or where key profit drivers are clearly beyond the control of the business unit, other financial measures can take the place of absolute profit as a goal in the marketing plan. In the auto industry, for example, commodity pricing and labor rates in large part set the costs. Since both of these items, are to some extent, outside the influence of the marketing team, or even the particular business unit, bottom-line profit is not an ideal goal. A better goal for a business unit, for example, might be revenue minus direct costs.

Similarly, the production cost of a feature film is basically fixed by the time it hits the theaters. As a result, the marketing plan for the film shouldn't focus too much on the production cost of the film; that is old news. Ticket pricing isn't in direct control of the marketing team; the price of a ticket to customers is set by the individual theaters. In this case, the marketing plan for the film should focus on driving ticket sales and getting people into the theaters to see the movie.

Revenue is a common—but flawed—goal. The advantage of having revenue as a goal in a marketing plan is that the link to marketing efforts is quite clear. Revenue, however, is rarely an ideal goal. In most businesses, revenue isn't the problem; profit is. With enough spending, any business can generate revenue. It might be unprofitable, but the revenue would come in. I could create a business with $10 million in revenue in about five minutes; I simply have to sell

$20 bills for $19. The sales would come in quickly and last until I ran out of money and had to shut down.

Other businesses are like this, too. It is not difficult at all to sell pasta at twenty-five cents a box. But it is hard to make any profit doing it. It is easy to discount the heck out of something and get some sales, but it is hard to make money that way. As Jim Owens, chairman and CEO of Caterpillar Inc., observed, "The Holy Grail is not top-line sales growth; it's bottom-line growth."[4]

Having a profit goal of some sort is a critical part of a marketing plan. As Tropicana marketer John Bauer explained, "People confuse a marketing plan and a communications plan. If you are not involved in the economics of the business, then all you have is a communications plan."

NONFINANCIAL GOALS

In many situations, a financial objective is not sufficient on its own; in this case, a marketing plan might have one or two other business objectives.

Most businesses must balance two forces. The first is short-term financial pressure, or the need to deliver the financial targets. This is critical for any organization. The second force is building a strong, enduring business through the creation of a differentiated brand and the strengthening of business capabilities.

Often these two forces fight each other. Moves to drive short-term profits are frequently harmful in the long term.

Examples of this are easy to see. Reducing quality to save a little product cost is a smart move to drive short-term profits, but long term, it is probably a very bad move, because customers will recognize that quality is eroding. Reducing advertising spending will likely help the short-term financial picture, but it will likely harm the brand later. Launching a new product is expensive; new products almost always lose money in the first year. A manager focused solely on a short-term financial target could cut funding for an important long-term new product initiative. By doing so, the manager would increase her odds of hitting the short-term target but fail with the new product.

Similarly, moves that build a brand and a strong business may well have a negative impact in the short run. Reducing the amount of discounting on a business will probably strengthen it in the long run by reducing the focus on price as a business driver. The move may well hurt short-term financial results. A major sponsorship program will have a limited short-term impact on sales and will probably hurt short-term profits, but it will strengthen the brand in the longer term.

As a result, a financial objective is often insufficient for a business; it suggests that the business can focus solely on the financials.

This is why many businesses have a broader business goal or two, in addition to a financial goal. This broader business goal provides guidance on the "how" in addition to the "what."

For example, a goal such as "Increase market share to 35 percent over the next twelve months" clearly highlights the importance of market share for the business. This is a particularly useful goal for a business that is experiencing fast growth; the business may easily deliver the financial targets while letting market share slide. In the long run, this could be a bad move. Having a market share goal ensures that market share is not neglected in the drive for short-term profits.

Take a goal such as "Improve customer satisfaction scores by 20 percent." By calling out this goal separately, the team understands that just driving profits isn't sufficient. The goal this year is to drive profits while boosting satisfaction.

THE GOOD, THE BAD, AND THE UGLY

Listed below are objectives from actual marketing plans. Some of these objectives work and others do not. It is useful to review why.

Beat the Competition

This is not a good objective. It is a good thought, of course. Anyone in business should aspire to beat the competition. The problem is that the objective is very vague. Beat the competition in what way?

"Beat the competition" can mean many different things. Beat the competition in unit market share, dollar marketing share, revenue, or profit? Beat the competition in what market, and what market segment?

In addition, this objective lacks a time element. By what date? It isn't clear when the competition will be beaten. An objective like this gives a manager a very easy out: "We'll get there next year."

Increase Operating Profit by 12 Percent versus Previous Year

This is a good objective. It is specific, measurable, relevant, and contains a time element. It is clear what the target is, and it will be simple to determine if the goal has been achieved or not.

Without knowing something about the business, it is impossible to assess whether the goal is realistic. But on the surface, a growth of 12 percent seems reasonable for an expanding company.

Invest in Quality

This is not a good objective. It is not specific or measurable, and it has no time element. What is quality, anyway? How do you measure it? A company could spend $50 improving something minor and claim it had invested in quality and achieved the goal.

On a more fundamental level, quality is not a great objective on its own. Quality is a means to an end; it isn't an end in itself. The question behind this objective is important: Why invest in quality? What is the goal behind the quality initiative?

It is hard to be opposed to quality, of course, but simply investing in quality is not a good objective.

Achieve Market Share Leadership in the Category by December 2014

This objective is on the right track. It is specific, presumably measurable, relevant, and mentions a specific time period. It will be clear at the end of 2014 whether or not you have reached the objective, and it is possible to measure progress toward the goal.

It is difficult to assess whether this objective is achievable without knowing the starting position and the broader business situation.

Reach $10 Billion in Sales in 2025

This objective has a clear goal and has a time element. The problem is that the objective is so far out in the future that it isn't relevant to the issues at hand. If you are creating a plan in early 2013, it is best to focus on 2013 and 2014. Looking out a dozen years is somewhat pointless; it isn't relevant at all to the questions that need to be addressed here and now in the marketing plan.

It is important to have a long-term vision for a business, of course, and a sense for where you want to go. But very distant goals should be part of a long-term planning exercise, not part of a marketing plan.

Objectives are not rallying cries or idle boasts. An objective should be a realistic, pragmatic goal.

APPROPRIATE EXPECTATIONS

Setting realistic objectives is more difficult than it might seem. Goals should be high enough to provide motivation but low enough to be achievable. Gladson CEO Mark Shapiro characterized it this way: "Numbers must be appropriately aggressive yet achievable."

Goals ultimately define success, so it is important to get them right. Is $100 million in profit a good result? Well, if the goal was $120 million, then $100 million is a poor outcome; the team finished well below plan. If the goal was $80 million, however, then $100 million is a terrific outcome; the team far exceeded the objectives.

Some people recommend stretch goals, or those that will be a real challenge to achieve. Better to reach for something and miss, the thinking goes, than to shoot too low. If you don't reach for the stars, you won't ever get them. A very high goal motivates people to do more and achieve more.

This line of thinking is fundamentally flawed. There is nothing wrong with firing up a team with big dreams. But exceptionally aggressive goals can create problems. First, high goals set teams up for disappointing results. To achieve the goals, the team must achieve remarkable results, and usually this won't happen. Missing objectives has several negative consequences: employees become discouraged, the sales team may lose motivation, and resources may be shifted to other more "successful" initiatives. As one marketer noted, "Adjusting plans downward in mid-year can cause inefficiency, loss of credibility, and poor morale." Missing goals also can result in programs being declared unsuccessful, when in reality the program was working fine. This results in rapid changes in programming, which is inefficient.

The other problem with stretch goals is that they can lead to dysfunctional behavior; in an effort to get to the incredibly difficult numbers, people and teams can focus on short-term levers, even if it hurts the business in the long run. If a team can achieve the goals only by burning the furniture, then there is a very real risk this will happen.

In extreme cases, stretch targets and big incentives can motivate employees to engage in unethical or illegal behavior. Bristol-Myers Squibb provides a vivid example of the dangers of high goals. Then-CEO Peter Dolan was a firm believer in setting high goals, or, as characterized in the management book *Built to Last*, "big, hairy, audacious goals." So Dolan set high targets and provided big incentives. Under his leadership, a number of senior executives manipulated the timing of product shipments to overstate short-term results; the company shipped product to distributors at the end of a fiscal year and booked the revenue, thereby apparently delivering strong results. In reality, of course, the sales were meaningless; they were simply pulled forward. Between 1999 and 2001, the company overstated revenues by $2.5 billion to meet quarterly sales targets.[5]

Objectives must reflect balance. As one marketing executive explained, good objectives are feasible: "They are relevant, they are doable, and they don't reach too far."

STRATEGIC INITIATIVES

The most important element of any great plan is the strategic initiatives. Although a plan is built to achieve objectives (and the objectives must be set first), the heart of a plan is its initiatives.

The strategic initiatives are what the business will do to achieve the objectives. These are the big ideas; they set the direction. As a result, this section should be the focus for people creating a plan and for the people reviewing it.

The terms "strategic initiative" and "strategy" can be used somewhat interchangeably, but I prefer the former because it makes it clear that the focus is on action. When people think about strategy, they often think broad, abstract thoughts that have very little to do with what the business will be doing over the next twelve months.

The most important thing to remember is that strategic initiatives are the steps a business takes toward what should be done. They are not the intended final outcome; that would be the objective. They are not a specific program recommendation; that would be a tactic. The strategic initiatives are the main actions. As Malcolm McDonald noted in his book *The Marketing Plan*, "An objective is what you want to achieve. A strategy is how you plan to achieve your objectives."[6]

NO TIME FOR PHILOSOPHY

Philosophy is a wonderful thing. It is good to think big thoughts and ponder on the meaning of life and other profound issues. It is also important; the big issues really do matter.

Big thoughts are also important when running a business. Long-term strategy is a good topic for consideration. Principles, too, play an important role in shaping a business.

The strategic initiatives in a marketing plan, however, are not the place for philosophical considerations. A strategic initiative should be precise and action oriented. It should state, in no uncertain terms, what needs to be done.

A good strategic initiative has several characteristics. First, it should be clear. The statement should use obvious language to explain precisely what is to be done. Second, a strategic initiative should be action oriented. It should usually start with a verb. Third, a good strategic initiative should be measurable, so that it is possible to evaluate if you are making headway against the initiative or not.

Fourth, a strategic initiative should directly support the objectives; there has to be linkage across the plan.

It is useful to consider different initiatives to understand what works best and why.

"Increase sales with heaviest users" could be a good strategic initiative. It is clear, action oriented, measurable, and presumably in support of the objectives.

Similarly, "attract new customers to the category" is a good strategic initiative. It is clear and direct. It is possible to measure progress. A team could easily develop tactics to support the initiative. Importantly, the tactics would be completely different from the tactics for increasing sales among existing users.

"Innovation" is not a good strategic initiative. Certainly, innovation is a good thing. Opposing innovation is a bit like opposing the environment; you really can't be against it. But on its own, innovation is just a word. It doesn't really say anything. What sort of innovation are we talking about? Is this a new product? Or is this a new cash management system? Or is this a way to make products for less?

Empty words lead to enormous problems. They sound good and seem to make sense. Who isn't in favor of innovation? The problem is that empty words don't actually say anything at all.

"Differentiate through added value" is another flawed strategy. It is action oriented, which is good. But it is terribly, hopelessly vague. It doesn't really say anything at all. They do more harm than good because they create uncertainty and confusion. Differentiate in what way? What type of added value are you considering? One marketing executive looked at this initiative and threw up his hands in disgust. He explained the problem: "It can mean a million different things."

"Run a coupon good for 30 cents off on August 4" is also not a good strategic initiative. It is simply a tactic. Although the phrase is clear, precise, and measurable, it is purely descriptive of a tactical marketing move. There is almost certainly a larger initiative behind this tactic, but it isn't readily apparent what that might be. To flesh out the real strategic initiative, the questions to ask are simple: What do we hope to accomplish with the coupon? Why are we doing this, anyway? How will it build sales?

It may be that the intent of the coupon is to get trial on a new product. In this case, the strategic initiative might be "Drive trial on the new product," or even broader, "Launch new product."

"Quality" is not a good strategic initiative. Much like innovation, quality is a very fine thing. It is hard to be against quality. But the word *quality* on its own says nothing. Are you improving product quality or reducing it? What is the action? What is the point? A better strategic initiative based on quality would be "improve service experience" or "address quality concerns."

THE POWER OF THREE

The inherent challenge in identifying strategic initiatives is that you can only have a few. If you could have two dozen initiatives, things would be simple. Indeed, most businesses would have pretty much the exact same list, highlighting everything one can do with a business. Things get difficult because a business can only focus on a few things. You have to choose.

Apple CEO Steve Jobs was a firm believer in focus. He explained it this way: "People think focus means saying yes to the thing you've got to focus on. But that's not what it means at all. It means saying no to the 100 other good ideas that there are. You have to pick carefully. I'm actually as proud of many of the things we haven't done as the things we have done."[7]

Great CEOs focus; they identify and communicate the top strategic initiatives. This is true across industries.

> I've moved to a place where I'm really focused on four things.
> —Ford CEO Alan Mulally[8]

> Since becoming President and CEO in 2005, I have focused on three strategic priorities.
> —Disney CEO Robert Iger[9]

As I mentioned in my letter last year, the UPS strategy has three key tenets.

—UPS CEO Scott Davis[10]

I have a great belief that you can't do more than five things.

—Abbott VP Mark Wheeler

The best number of strategic initiatives for a business is three. This is true whether the business is small or large.

Having three strategic initiatives provides two benefits. First, it forces great focus, and focus is essential for getting things done. The truth is that although we like to think we can do lots of things at the same time, we can't. As Adobe's Mark Delman observed, "You can only get an organization to do a couple things in any given year." AspireUp's Roland Jacobs is also a believer in the power of three, noting, "Even the most complex business should have three things it's focused on."

Second, it is easy to communicate and remember three things. People tend to remember things in groups of threes and fours—which is likely why phone numbers in many nations are broken into groups of three or four numbers.

It is possible to have four strategic initiatives, or even five, and still retain some focus. Each additional initiative, however, subtracts from the overall impact of the plan.

Eight strategic initiatives are too many; they are just a list of things to do. It is impossible to focus on eight things. The same is true for eleven, fourteen, and seventeen; the complexity is too great.

Having just one or two initiatives is also not good, because it doesn't provide much texture. If a business has just one or two strategic initiatives, they are most likely very broad. For example, a company that outlines the two initiatives of "build unit sales" and "build margins" isn't saying very much at all; the strategic initiatives are all-encompassing; almost everything falls into one bucket or the other. Similarly, a plan with the initiatives of "build sales with existing customers" and "build sales with new customers" is adding little value; it would be simpler to say "build sales," because the two broad strategic initiatives include everyone, anyway.

Researchers at Eli Lilly recently completed a study that highlighted the importance of communicating just a few things. The study looked at the communication of drug side effects. What happened, the researchers wondered, as a company communicated more side effects about a drug? Would people actually remember a greater number of them? Or was being thorough and including more side effects actually counterproductive, such that people tended to remember fewer of them?

In the study, the researchers created three different versions of the same print ad. One version of the ad included four side effects, another version of the ad included eight side effects, and the final version of the ad included twelve side effects. The researchers then showed the ads to consumers and evaluated what people remembered.

Surprisingly, the study showed that increasing the number of side effects in the ad did not result in consumers remembering more. Instead, the reverse happened; increasing the number of side effects in the ad meant that people actually remembered fewer. Consumers on average remembered 1.04 side effects when shown an ad that listed four side effects, and consumers remembered only 0.85 side effects when shown an ad with twelve side effects. This suggests that when people see more information, they remember less on a percentage basis, and less in the absolute.

In addition, as the number of side effects listed in the ad increased, more people failed to remember any of them at all. With four side effects, 36 percent of consumers couldn't remember even one. With eight side effects, the portion of consumers who couldn't remember any of them increased to 45 percent. With twelve side effects, a remarkable 53 percent of consumers could not remember even one of the side effects. This suggests that the more data people see, the more likely they are to forget everything.[11]

Of course, this really is just common sense. Long lists are difficult to absorb; people quickly get overwhelmed and forget all of the items. Recently, I went to a talk on the eleven keys to successful branding. The talk was quite interesting, and the speaker had some very good points. But after the talk I couldn't remember any of the points; there were so many different things to keep track of, I lost track of them all. I had to go back to my notes to remember the list. And then, when I was asked later about the talk, I was able to recall only a few things.

A marketing plan should never have a dozen initiatives. This not only indicates a lack of focus; more importantly, it virtually guarantees the plan will not be memorable. The audience is likely to be overwhelmed, and this is not a positive.

Having ten strategic initiatives is perhaps worst of all. It is too many for people to remember, and the number is so round and even that it seems like the plan was simply stretched or compressed to make things neat and tidy.

Paring down and focusing on three strategic initiatives is difficult, but it is the heart of the marketing plan process and will help bring your company the most success. Indeed, if you're not able to distill the plan down into the most important strategies, the work isn't done. One executive noted that getting down to three strategies is critical, explaining, "If you can't focus it that much, you don't really have a strategy."

Strategic initiatives come from analysis and from thinking. A manager must be able to take all the information available and distill it down into the most important factors. As Nestlé's Stephen Cunliffe observed, "You need to be able to synthesize a lot of material and turn it into some logical strategies."

When selecting the initiatives, it is useful to think about the phrase "mutually exclusive, collectively exhaustive" (MECE). Many consulting firms find this concept useful when writing recommendations. "Mutually exclusive" means that each item should be distinct, with minimal overlap. "Collectively exhaustive" means that, combined, the initiatives should address the main issues and be sufficient to achieve the objectives.

TACTICS

Tactics are specific actions: the programs and the ideas that will bring the strategic initiatives to life. The tactics lay out precisely what will be done. A strategy sets the overall direction, and the tactic provides the specific execution plan. Put another way, the strategic initiatives highlight what needs to happen, and the tactics show how it will be done.

Tactics include advertising campaigns, sponsorships, promotions, and product improvements. Tactics are sales efforts, public relations campaigns, and social media programs. Tactics are the details.

For example, Nike might pursue the strategic initiative of "Gain share and establish credibility in soccer." The tactics supporting this initiative could include identifying and sponsoring promising young soccer stars, introducing a new line of high-end soccer footwear, and expanding retail presence of the soccer line.

Of course, only the most important tactics should be highlighted in a marketing plan; the goal is to focus on the most critical things. Every product has a price, for example, but pricing should only show up in a marketing plan if pricing is particularly important as a tactic.

Every strategic initiative should have tactics. Indeed, an initiative without tactics is a red flag; if an initiative doesn't have specific actions associated with it, the odds are that nothing will happen. The intent is there, but the action is not.

Similarly, each tactic should be related to a broader strategic initiative. A strategy and a tactic should have a direct connection between them. For any tactic, the questions that have to be asked are simple: Why are we doing this? What strategic initiative does it support?

If a tactic isn't connected to an initiative, a manager should take a second look at the tactic. Is it really that important? And if it is important, why is that the case? What is the initiative behind the tactic? Is there really another strategic initiative the tactic is driving? If so, should it replace one of those currently highlighted in the plan?

Being disciplined about linking tactics to strategic initiatives is fundamental to a marketing plan's success. It is through the process of focusing on the most important tactics that a plan takes life. As Johnson & Johnson's Sharon D'Agostino observed, "The key is being relentless in doing just what you say you're going to do. If it isn't consistent with the strategy, we aren't going to do it."

THE FOUR Ps AT LAST

Tactics are where the familiar four Ps—product, price, promotion, and place (or distribution)—should appear in a marketing plan.

In most cases, the four Ps are not strategic initiatives. Promotion alone is rarely a strategic initiative; promotion should be thought of as a means to accomplish something specific, which will in turn drive sales. For example, a coupon might be focused on driving trial on a new product, and this supports the overall objective of building revenue and profit. Similarly, distribution programs need to be viewed in the larger context; a distribution drive is usually done to achieve something specific, which will ultimately drive sales and profit.

Anyone who looks upon the four Ps as strategic initiatives in and of themselves is likely to encounter problems; the plan will end up being very tactical, lacking integration across the different elements.

For example, if the overall goals are to drive profit and share growth, a strategic initiative might be to attract competitors' customers. The tactics supporting this initiative might then span the four Ps. For example, one tactic might be using advertising to encourage people to compare the products (promotion). Another tactic could be cutting prices to match competition (price). Another might be to expand distribution in key geographic areas (place).

THE ONE-PAGE SUMMARY

A marketing plan can be summarized on one page by laying out the goals (objectives), strategic initiatives, and tactics. The objectives lead to the initiatives, and the initiatives lead to the tactics.

Exhibit 4.1   GOST Framework

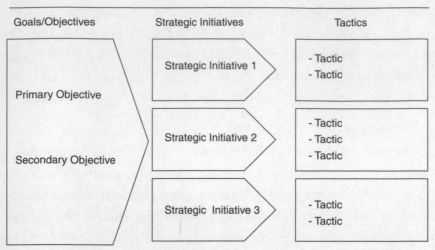

This one-page summary is a powerful tool and should be part of every marketing plan. It does three things particularly well.

First, it forces a manager to focus. There isn't room for eight strategies and twenty-seven tactics. There is only room for one or two objectives, three or four strategies, and two or three tactics for each strategy. This means that a manager must go through the process of selecting the most important things.

Second, it provides an easy way to check that the plan holds together and is internally consistent. By seeing all the key elements on one page, it is easy to test whether the plan is linked. Obvious problems surface quickly. For example, if a strategic initiative has no tactics, it is almost certain that nothing will happen against that initiative. If there are tactics that don't fall under any strategic initiative, the plan may not be focused or complete. If there are many initiatives, the plan is not yet tight.

Third, the one-page summary is a wonderful plan recap. This chart, placed at the end of a marketing plan, will summarize all the activities held within the plan itself. This makes it a powerful communication device.

It is important to note, however, that the one page is not a complete plan; it is simply the summary. It doesn't include the rationale supporting the plan, and it doesn't address financial issues. As a result, just completing the chart is not sufficient; you need the rest of the plan wrapped around it.

*   *   *

A marketing plan really needs just three things. The first is the goals, or objectives—in other words, what the business is trying to achieve. The second is the strategic initiatives, or the three or four big moves the business will make in order to achieve growth. The third is the tactics, or the specific programs and moves the business will make to support the strategic initiatives. It really is strikingly simple.

Chapter 5

THE BEST MARKETING PLANS

WHILE RESEARCHING THIS BOOK, I asked dozens of marketers the same question: "Tell me about the best marketing plan you have ever seen. What made it so good?" Whether they worked in pharmaceuticals or financial services or consumer packaged goods, whether they worked for a nonprofit or a for-profit organization, and whether they worked in the United States or Asia, their answers were all the same.

It isn't entirely surprising that what works in one industry works in another, because marketing plans are always about people, both externally (customers) and internally (the business team and senior management).

The best marketing plans have four things in common, which can be summarized by the acronym FACS: they are focused, achievable, compelling, and simple.

FOCUS

Focus is the most important characteristic of a good marketing plan; a great plan concentrates on the most important initiatives and the most important tactics.

The challenge for managers today isn't to identify things that are good to do, or things that would help grow sales. That is a fairly simple task. The challenge is picking the few things that will really matter, the things that will have a major impact on the business.

Great plans highlight the most important priorities for the business and don't get bogged down by including everything. The best marketing plans will embrace focus. The plan will highlight what has to happen, why it is important, and how it will occur.

For most businesses, just a few things really matter at any given point. There are many details to manage, of course. Shipments must go out, supplies must be ordered, customers must be billed, and taxes must be filed. But success, or failure, will stem from just a few big initiatives. Understanding this is essential; a manager who knows that just a few things really matter can focus intensely on those things.

Dell Computer founder Michael Dell credits much of his company's success to developing strong business plans with focus. He observed in a 2005 interview, "For the past decade, we've identified three major objectives every year—the same initiatives, supported by the same metrics, everywhere in the world." He continued, "A lot of our success is due to the fact that we've been able to pick the right things at the right time and align the entire worldwide organization around them. They help the entire organization stay focused on what we're trying to accomplish."[1] Jeff Immelt, CEO of General Electric, noted similarly in a 2004 interview, "Every leader needs to clearly explain the top three things the organization is working on. If you can't, then you're not leading well."[2]

Marketing plans should operate at a high level with a focus on the big strategic initiatives and then the most important tactics. Beware, though, that it is easy to get bogged down in the tactical details of the plan; all sorts of interesting things can be said about any particular promotion or pricing plan. Indeed, it is great fun to present the ins and outs of a new and exciting program. Even the most mundane of marketing tactics, a coupon in the Sunday morning paper, can lead to all sorts of thought-provoking and sometimes controversial discussions.

What is the value of the coupon? Should it be good off two items, or good off only one? When and where will it run? When do you expect the competitors to have coupons? Do you want to be before them or after? How much time until the coupon expires? Why? What products will be featured in the picture? What color is the background?

The problem, of course, is that all these questions are relatively unimportant. Tactical plans tend to be long, detailed, and ultimately not productive. The big issues are never addressed, and the tactical questions and issues dominate the discussion. Instead of talking about the growth drivers of the business or ways to deal with a major competitive threat, a tactical marketing plan wastes time on small, unimportant programs, such as the sampling program in Omaha or the PR event in Frankfurt. It misses the point.

The process of focusing is difficult because the marketer must filter and prioritize, including only the recommendations and data that truly have an impact on the business. As Jim Kilts, former CEO of Nabisco and Gillette, observed, "Regardless of your position in a company or organization, there is always a flood of information and data, and a lot of conflicting ideas and opinions. In the end, how you get to the heart of the matter will define you as a leader."[3]

Focusing is challenging because the world is full of interesting and relevant information. Of course, people filter all the time. Barry Schwartz, author of *The Paradox of Choice: Why More is Less*, observed that cutting out irrelevant information is something people do all the time. According to Schwartz, "Filtering out extraneous information is one of the basic functions of consciousness. If everything available to our senses demanded our attention at all times, we wouldn't be able to get through the day."[4] Marketing plans are similar; if an executive included all the possible details in a plan, no one would ever be able to read it.

Marketing veteran Sergio Pereira points out that focused plans show that the manager knows the business. He says, "A great plan makes it easy to tell that people have figured out the things that matter and the things that don't."

ACHIEVABLE

At one point in my career, I was promoted to run a dynamic new business. The business had just ended its second year in the market, a year marked by sharp increases in sales volume and market share. After meeting the team, I sat down to review the marketing plan and was rather dismayed by what I read.

I quickly realized that the business had been growing quickly because of very high levels of spending in both advertising and promotions; all the promotion activity on the business had helped it steal share from competitors despite its being a largely commodity item.

The marketing plan for the following year called for further growth in share and sales but a sharp reduction in spending. The theory was that after two years of introductory support, the business had enough momentum to continue growing without so much spending.

The problem was that the marketing plan was not based at all on reality. Cutting support on a product that had sold mainly because it had been heavily promoted was not going to result in continued growth. Instead, the business would collapse.

The marketing plan, in other words, was a purely fictional document, built on either a lack of understanding or, as it turned out, a heavy dose of wishful thinking. It was totally unachievable.

A great marketing plan has to be built on realistic assumptions. It has to be achievable based on the dynamics in the market. A marketing plan built on unrealistic assumptions adds little value. It is a bit like doing a financial plan based on winning the lottery; it all looks great but is not likely to happen. As Barry Sternlicht, former chairman and CEO of Starwood Hotels and Resorts Worldwide, noted, "When you start making decisions based on what you wish were true, you're going to make some pretty bad calls."[5]

Aggressive targets can actually create significant problems. There is a good chance the business will fall behind the plan. When this happens, managers will be tempted to focus on short-term levers to try to boost results and get back on track. So they might cut the advertising budget and add a big new promotion. This will likely drive up sales in the short run, but in the long term the business will weaken as customers become accustomed to the lower prices and as the brand equity fades. As Procter & Gamble CEO A. G. Lafley explained, "Once a company starts pursuing unrealistic growth objectives, it will rarely, if ever, create the capability and flexibility to invest in long-term growth. Instead it will borrow from the future to sustain the present."[6]

In a strong marketing plan, objectives are achievable, and the strategic initiatives and tactics are feasible. The plan has to be credible.

Every marketing plan should have a section on financials, as these play a critical role in the planning process. Indeed, as Unilever veteran David Hirschler remarked, "The financials are the most important part."

Ultimately, a marketing plan has to work financially. The spending on the business has to drive sufficient revenue to deliver the needed profit. In particular, a clear link should exist between the recommended strategic initiatives and the financials. If the business succeeds at executing the initiatives, will the business deliver the financial targets? Why or why not? One marketing leader explained the situation by saying, "It is one thing to say you want to grow 10 percent a year. It is another to really understand how you will get there."

To show how a business *will* get there, a marketing plan should include basic, realistic financial projections, showing the outlook for the business and the ways in which the strategies will translate into results. This is essential to ensure that the marketing plan will deliver the needed objectives. As one general manager observed, "I can't image a marketing plan without a P&L. It's theory without the P&L."

Ignoring the financial outlook for a business is an enormous miss; it overlooks the key objective and doesn't highlight how the recommended strategies and tactics link to the results. As Tropicana's John Bauer explained, "The P&L links the spending to the business."

COMPELLING

A great marketing plan is compelling; someone reading or hearing the plan should walk away convinced that the recommendations make sense and are the best available. Because a primary goal of a marketing plan is to gain support, the plan must be convincing to be successful. Stephen Cunliffe, president of the frozen foods division at Nestlé USA, has reviewed hundreds of marketing plans over the course of his career. He noted that great plans leave a reviewer feeling comfortable with the plan and the team, saying, "These guys know where they're going, and I have confidence."

Many marketing plans fall short in this area. A plan might explain what needs to be done but not how it will all happen. It isn't convincing.

In order to be convincing, a plan must explain why the recommendations make sense. It also must highlight why the objectives are correct and why the strategies will work to achieve the objectives.

A plan also must deal proactively with potential questions or issues. A great marketing plan highlights alternative strategies and the reasons they will not work as well as the plan's final recommendation. A marketer writing an excellent plan anticipates obvious questions and answers them.

To be compelling, a plan must be based in data and analysis. Facts are indisputable, and they provide reason for someone to believe in the recommendation. In a sense, facts are the foundation on which a great marketing plan is built.

SIMPLE

Great marketing plans are simple. The issues are apparent, the strategies make sense, and the tactics clearly show the execution of the strategies. The rationale supports the points. It is clear why the data is being presented and what it means. As Margaret Stender, president and CEO of the professional women's basketball team the Chicago Sky, observed, "We've got to challenge ourselves to find a way to keep it simple."[7]

In the most successful marketing plans, the facts fit together, the points flow logically from one to the next, and the strategies build to tactics and to the financial implications. It all feels simple and intuitive. Someone reading the plan might say, "Well, of course. This is obviously what we should be doing. It won't be easy, but the plan makes sense."

Simplicity is important since one of the main reasons managers write marketing plans is to get approval and support for their recommendations. Before someone can support something, of course, he or she must understand it. A simple plan, then, is critical for getting people on board. As Joseph Jimenez, CEO of Novartis, observes, "I personally believe that if you can't hold something in your head, then you're not going to be able to internalize it and act on it. At Novartis, our business is very complicated. But you have to distill the strategy down to its essence for how we're going to win, and what we're really going to go after, so that people can hold it in their heads."[8]

It is tempting to assume that complicated and data-intensive plans are those most likely to receive support. Some people seem to think that if they include everything, others will see all the information and agree with their conclusion. This is flawed logic. If people can't understand the plan, or don't finish reading it, they are not likely to support it.

Most businesses are fundamentally simple. The strategies that drive them are not difficult to follow. Things become complex only when the details are added. As General Electric's Jack Welch observed, "People always over-estimate how complex business is. This isn't rocket science; we've chosen one of the world's more simple professions. Most global businesses have three or four critical competitors, and you know who they are. And there aren't that many things you can do with a business. It's not as if you're choosing among 2,000 options."[9]

Recent academic research studies have shown the importance of simplicity. Two of the more interesting studies were conducted by professors Sheena Iyengar and Mark Lepper and published in the *Journal of Personality and Social Psychology*.

In the first study, Iyengar and Lepper set up a table in a grocery store and invited people to sample different high-end jams. At certain times, they offered consumers six different jams. At other times, they offered twenty-four different jams.

The results were striking. When more jams were offered, more people stopped to try the jam (60 percent as opposed to 40 percent), which indicated that a larger selection initially was more appealing. Few people who stopped, however, ultimately purchased a jam when forced to decide among twenty-four different options. Only 3 percent of people who stopped at the table with twenty-four different jams bought one. Conversely, almost 30 percent of the people who stopped at the table with six different jams made a purchase. The results seemed to contradict common sense that people would embrace options and choice.

The key insight, however, is that more isn't always better. Twenty-four jams were simply too many; consumers were overwhelmed by the selection and couldn't make a decision, and so they walked away without making a purchase.

In another study, Iyengar and Lepper had consumers taste Godiva chocolate. Participants could choose from either six or thirty different varieties. Iyengar and Lepper then studied how well the consumers liked the chocolate and simulated a purchase by letting participants choose between money and chocolate in return for participating in the study.

Once again, the results were clear—and counterintuitive. Consumers who chose among fewer chocolates generally liked the chocolate better (average satisfaction of 6.3 versus 5.5) and were more inclined to ultimately purchase the chocolate by choosing the chocolate instead of the money (48 percent versus 12 percent). Tellingly, consumers who chose between the thirty chocolates later had a sense of regret about the experience.[10]

The research by Iyengar and Lepper highlights the importance of simplicity. Making things complicated often makes them less appealing. More data isn't better, more choice isn't better, more options aren't better. A great marketing plan takes all the data and all the research and boils it down into the key initiatives. As Tropicana's John Bauer observed, "It's all about synthesizing the data to find the relevant information."

But simplicity isn't simple! Identifying the key priorities is hard; you have to eliminate many very good options. Most people don't like making choices. It is easy to add things and create complexity. It is hard to trim, cutting everything that is interesting but not essential. As Apple's Steve Jobs observed, "It takes a lot of hard work to make something simple, to truly understand the underlying challenges and come up with elegant solutions."[11]

*   *   *

The characteristics of a great marketing plan are universal; they are focused, achievable, compelling, and simple. Anyone creating a marketing plan should test the plan against these criteria. Before presenting your plan, look at it and ask a few basic questions. Is it focused on just a few big things? Can we really achieve the goals? Is it presented in a compelling way? Is it simple to read and understand?

Asking these basic questions will ensure that the plan is on the right track.

Chapter 6

THE PLANNING PROCESS

CREATING A BREAKTHROUGH MARKETING PLAN takes time, energy, and effort. You can't just sit down and write a marketing plan in an hour, unless you are working in a very small organization and already know the business exceptionally well. A good plan is based on a deep understanding of the business, the customer, the competition, and the market, together with smart strategic thinking and solid program development. All of this takes time.

It can be difficult to know where to start because in almost every case there are many issues to address and piles and piles of data to work with. The questions, and the potential solutions, go on and on.

Starting in the wrong spot can lead to trouble. Action-oriented people will tend to begin the marketing plan process by thinking about tactical moves and specific programs. "We need a new advertising campaign!" they might exclaim as they kick off the process. Or, "We should run our summer promotion early this year to preempt the competition!" This is a tempting approach, but it is rarely successful. You should make specific tactical decisions—such as advertising spending, packaging changes, and the timing of promotions—after the overall plan is clear. It makes little sense to talk about advertising creative, for example, until there is agreement on the role and purpose of advertising in the overall plan.

Thoughtful, analytical people may begin the marketing planning process by studying the business and understanding the ins and outs of the market; they will look at recent results, trends, competitive moves, changes in the channel, and consumer shifts. This approach is conceptually fine. After all, a good plan should be grounded in analysis. But starting the process by studying the business leads to problems, too; the amount of analysis one can do on a business is virtually unlimited, so there is a very real risk that the entire process will get bogged down in this step.

This chapter presents an eight-step process for creating a breakthrough marketing plan. The approach is appropriate for both small and large businesses; consider it your road map to success in creating your own breakthrough marketing plan.

STEP 1: CREATE A CROSS-FUNCTIONAL TEAM

It is impossible to create a marketing plan on your own. You need to get your cross-functional peers involved in the process. This point was highlighted for me several years ago when I sat in on the annual plan presentation for a $500-million business. The category director was enthusiastic, and she was delighted with her team's plan.

At the end of the two-hour meeting, she wrapped up with a big, high-energy finish: "We are incredibly excited about this plan and think we have a terrific year ahead. Thank you for your time and attention. Now the team will be happy to take your questions!"

The room fell silent for a minute while the audience digested all the material. Then from the back came the first comment. It was from the vice president of sales. "This is all well and good, but it won't work, you know. You can't reallocate trade spending across markets; we have too many national accounts to do that."

The category director paused and then commented, "But reallocating trade spending lets us reduce our spending, and this in turn lets us invest in the additional advertising we are counting on to build the brand."

The VP of sales frowned. "I understand what you want to do. I'm just saying you can't do it. It won't work."

And with that, a hush fell over the room.

"Why don't we take this off-line?" said the category director, seizing the one emergency ripcord available. It was the only possible way out. But the energy from the presentation was gone, and everyone in the audience knew it. The category director had failed to involve critical people in the decision-making process during the writing of the marketing plan, and as a result the entire plan was built on incorrect assumptions.

Creating a marketing plan is a cross-functional activity. The decisions in the marketing plan affect many parts of the organization; they have an impact on marketing, research, sales, R&D, human resources, and finance, among other groups. As a result, many functions should provide input and must ultimately agree with the plan and the recommendations.

In most cases, a particular person or department is responsible for leading the planning process; this might be the brand manager or the marketing vice president or even the general manager. This is good; having a clear leader is important because ownership is essential. But that leader can't do it alone.

As a result, the first step in developing a marketing plan is simple but frequently overlooked: Assemble the cross-functional team that will create the plan.

There are two reasons to start by creating a cross-functional team. First, this will lead to a better plan. A good marketing plan will touch all parts of a business and consider issues that directly affect almost every function. This includes new products, advertising, pricing, sales, customer service, public relations, quality control, and production planning. The list goes on and on. A marketing plan that doesn't at least refer to R&D efforts, for example, will be less than optimal. Similarly, a plan that doesn't consider product quality and product cost will be incomplete.

As a result, it is essential to involve the cross-functional team in the marketing planning process. It is very hard to discuss issues related to the sales force, for example, without involvement from the sales organization. It is similarly difficult to discuss new product development without the participation of the R&D group. Cross-functional team members bring insights and knowledge and ideas. If it is impossible to implement a packaging change, for example, it is best to know this early in the process.

Indeed, if the only people working on a marketing plan are the people who work in marketing, that's a problem. The final product will fall far short of its potential; it will either only address core marketing topics such as advertising and promotions, or it will not have the needed information.

The second reason to form a cross-functional team is to build support. The best way to get someone's approval is to involve that person in the decision-making process. It's easy to criticize a plan you didn't create. It's harder to criticize a plan you created; if there were problems, why didn't you address them?

Excluding a particularly influential player from the marketing planning process is a big risk; this person may well find problems later. More significant, he or she may feel resentful or even angry at being left out and may find fault with the marketing plan when it is presented. In the unfortunate story above, it is clear that the sales group was not involved in creating the plan. As a result, the plan was based on an assumption about trade spending that was fundamentally flawed.

Making sure various functions are represented is not enough, however; you have to be careful to get the right people. This is a bit of an art. Having senior people on the team is good because they bring knowledge and insight. Frequently, however, they will not have time to participate in the process; they will miss meetings and never fully engage. Junior people may have more time and motivation but lack the necessary credibility. Balance is important; you need people with enough experience to contribute but also people able and willing to spend time on the task.

When creating the team, a leader should identify the key players, gather them together, lay out the plan, and secure commitment to the task.

In reality, not every member of the team will be equally involved; some are there to provide input and give buy-in rather than to take the lead in writing the plan. Nonetheless, involving people early and often will ensure that the final plan deals with obvious issues and has cross-functional support.

STEP 2: CHECK THE FOUNDATION

You can't build a strong house on a weak foundation, and the same is true for a marketing plan; you can't create a breakthrough plan if the fundamentals are not in place. Before you can develop a marketing plan, you need to understand what the business is built on in the first place.

As a result, the second step in the process is to check the foundation of the business in order to confirm the long-term direction. This step is often just a routine check to ensure that the foundation is still solid and strong. Sometimes, however, it becomes clear that there is no foundation, or that it is unstable. In this case, there is more work to do—but not on the marketing plan.

Marketing plans are by nature relatively short-term vehicles; the focus is on the next one or two or, at the most, three years. Marketing plans are not long-term strategic planning documents; a marketing plan should address what the business will do in the immediate future. A marketing plan with a ten-year horizon is so broad and vague that it does little to address the immediate questions of what should be done now—and why.

Brands and businesses, however, have a much longer horizon. Brands can live decades or centuries. Ford was founded in 1903. Gucci started in 1921. Coke first appeared in 1886. Starbucks, though it seems like an overnight success story, dates back to 1971.

Indeed, most of the value of a business lies far in the future; the next one or two years are important, but what really matters is the next decade, and the one after that. Simply looking at a basic net present value calculation highlights this; if you use a 5 percent discount rate and value a business that produces a flat stream of cash flows, you quickly realize that the next year accounts for only 5 percent of the value of the business. The value lies in the future.

As a result, the marketing planning process must be created with a sense of the larger picture. Any decision on a business has to be made with an appreciation of the long term; this provides context. Decisions in the next one or two years must move the organization toward its long-term goal and must also build on the past.

By reviewing the core direction of a business up front, the team can understand longer-term objectives and developing opportunities. In addition, understanding the foundation of the business lowers the risk that the final plan will be inconsistent with the long-term direction of the organization.

For example, deciding to increase prices at Walmart might appear to be a sound idea to increase margins and profits. However, the Walmart brand is built on giving customers low prices; if prices increase, then the entire brand positioning changes. Similarly, deciding to launch a high-performance convertible might be a way for Volvo to drive incremental sales, but the move would be inconsistent with Volvo's core positioning of safety. This would make little sense.

You should focus on two things in particular in this stage of the process: brand positioning and company vision. These are quite different, and both are important. Positioning defines what a brand means. Vision describes what an organization hopes to achieve over the long run; it provides a sense of purpose and the big picture.

Every business should have a vision and a brand positioning. These are two basic, fundamental tools. It is difficult to lead an organization without understanding its long-term goals, and it is difficult to manage a brand without understanding its positioning.

In most cases, this step in developing the marketing plan is simply a process of assembling the materials. Both vision and positioning should remain fairly constant from year to year, so the focus should not be on changing either one unless absolutely necessary.

If one or the other doesn't exist, however, or is clearly off, this step becomes more complicated and will require some work. It is time well spent because setting a strong foundation for the marketing plan is critically important. A house built on a weak foundation may look nice while it is being built, but it will ultimately crumble. Similarly, a marketing plan built without a sense of the bigger picture usually will miss the mark.

POSITIONING

A brand is a set of associations linked to a name, mark, or symbol. A brand is everything that pops into your head when you think of a product. When you think about BMW, for example, you may think performance, technology, Germany, and expensive. When you think about McDonald's, you may think kids, French fries, quick, golden arches, and red.

The difference between a name and a brand is simple. A name without associations is just a name. For example, Claire's Cola doesn't mean a lot. Coca-Cola, however, has all sorts of associations, making it a brand.

Brands matter because people never see just a product; they see a product and a brand. The brand functions as a lens that changes how people see the product. People see the product specifications, of course, but these are shaped by the brand. Vodka, a colorless, odorless, and tasteless liquid, becomes very special when one puts the Grey Goose brand on it. In the United States, a perfectly fine automobile may take on negative quality associations when linked with General Motors.

Great marketers understand that shaping the associations around a brand is a key business challenge. A strong brand will help a product for many, many years. A negative or weak brand will hurt.

Positioning is an essential tool for managing a brand. It is grounded in a very simple insight: Great brands are tightly defined. The best brands stand for something distinct. In the world of automobiles, Volvo stands for safety, BMW stands for performance, Rolls-Royce stands for luxury, and Honda stands for reliable quality.

A brand cannot be all things to all people. Indeed, the more it tries to appeal to everyone, the more a brand loses what makes it distinct; in an effort to broaden its appeal, a brand becomes more and more general.

Positioning is a tool for clarifying how a brand will compete in the market; it states the intended meaning of a brand. Ideally, a brand's positioning is the same as its associations in the market. Sometimes this is not the case; a company might want the brand to mean one thing, but it actually means something else. This highlights the need for more work to ensure that the brand means what the company wants it to mean.

Brand positioning has four essential parts: target, frame of reference, primary benefit, and key attribute.

The first part of a positioning is target, or who the brand is for. This is usually based on a market segmentation study and is almost always grounded in a deep insight into the customer. The target in positioning does not need to include everyone who buys the brand; it should simply specify for whom the brand is intended.

The second part is the frame of reference, or what the brand really is. This can be thought of as the competitive set. Sometimes this is obvious. Steinway, for example, is a brand of high-end piano. Taco Bell is a fast-food restaurant. Absolut is a brand of vodka. Sometimes, though, this question is less obvious. What, precisely, is Yahoo!? Having a clear frame of reference is important; it is hard to explain to someone why to buy something if you don't first tell them what it is.

The third part of a positioning is the primary benefit, or the most important reason for the target to buy the product. The key thing to remember when it comes to positioning is that a brand can have only one benefit. Brands that try to be many things all at the same time end up causing confusion.

The final part of the positioning is the reason why. This should support the primary benefit; the reason why provides the evidence points that justify the positioning. A brand can have one or two or even three reasons why. All of them, however, should support the positioning.

The four elements of a positioning can be presented in a simple statement that combines all the parts. The statement follows a simple format.

> To (target),
> X is the brand of (frame of reference)
> that (primary benefit)
> because (key attributes).

A brand positioning statement should work as a single thought. The target should value the benefit. The benefit should be relevant and clearly delineated within the frame of reference. The reasons why should support the benefit.

When written out, a brand positioning can look something like this:

> To serious athletes,
> Nike is the brand of athletic equipment and apparel
> that lets you perform your very best
> because Nike products are made with the latest and best technology and design.

> To people who know and appreciate fine coffee,
> Peet's is the brand of premium coffee
> that has the most robust taste
> because Peet's is roasted daily by people who are passionate about coffee.

A positioning statement is not a slogan; it is a tool to be used internally to help define the intended meaning of a brand. It feels clunky in a self-conscious sort of way when written out; it's not poetry. But a positioning statement is a powerful way to summarize what a brand means.

A brand may also have a character statement in addition to positioning. Positioning is how a brand competes with other players in the market. Character describes the personality of the brand.

If brand positioning is all about differentiation, brand character is all about spirit. It is not necessary for a brand character to be unique, but a brand character should capture the essence of the brand. For example, the Tiffany brand character might include words such as *classic*, *elegant*, *refined*, *traditional*, and *romantic*.

Every brand should have a positioning. If an organization has twelve different brands, it should also have twelve different positioning statements and twelve brand character statements to accompany them.

VISION

Vision sets the long-term direction for a business; it speaks to the big question of what an organization wants to achieve in the long run. In a sense, vision answers the age-old question, "So what do you want to be when you grow up?" As Jim Collins and Jerry Porras wrote in their classic 1996 article on vision, "Companies that enjoy enduring success have core values and a core purpose that remain fixed while their business strategies and practices endlessly adapt to a changing world."[1]

It is highly unlikely that a series of one- or two-year plans will lead a business to its long-term goal. A company that wants to be the quality leader may not actually achieve this goal if the business team focuses only on optimizing plans for next year. The focus each year might be on using promotions to drive volume and cost reductions to prop up profits. This plan might deliver some solid financial results in the short run, but it certainly won't achieve the long-term objective.

As a result, a business team needs to approach a marketing plan with a sense of the greater goal and the greater purpose. The marketing plan then needs to build toward the long-term goals.

You should consider three particularly important things when formulating a vision. The first is the statement of purpose, or what the organization actually does. For example, according to Procter & Gamble CEO A. G. Lafley, his company's purpose is simple, "We create products and services that improve everyday life."

The second is company values, or what is important to the organization. Dell recently went through a process of defining its values. According to CEO Kevin Rollins, "That led us to define the soul of Dell: focus on the customer, be open and direct in communications, be a good corporate citizen, have fun in winning."[2]

The third important part of vision is a long-term objective, or what the organization wants to achieve over a sustained period of time. This often takes the form of an inspirational statement. For example, Teen Living Programs, a nonprofit organization dedicated to helping homeless teens in Chicago, has embraced this statement: "Teen Living Programs will be a model agency for the world, a shining example of a provider of services to youth who are homeless, recognized as a national leader in moving youth from homelessness to permanent independence."

Jim Collins and Jerry Porras refer to this as the envisioned future, the somewhat unreachable destination. "We recognize that the phrase *envisioned future* is somewhat paradoxical. On the one hand, it conveys concreteness—something visible, vivid, and real. On the other hand, it involves a time yet unrealized—with its dreams, hopes, and aspirations."[3]

Visions can take many forms. Some are long and detailed; others are very simple. I recently visited a modest barbeque restaurant near my office. There, taped to the wall on faded paper, was the following statement:

> What We're About
> Giving our customers the best BBQ anywhere
> Doing it with fun, flair, excellence, and excitement
> Serving our customers

A simple statement, indeed, but one that captures what the organization is about; it conveys a sense of focus and values.

Simple or complex, basic or elegant, it is essential to have something that sets the long-term direction for a business, because a marketing plan always needs to be created with a sense of perspective.

STEP 3: CLARIFY THE GOALS AND OBJECTIVES

"We're going to restart this business!" proclaimed the dynamic new division general manager of Kraft's struggling grocery division. "We have harvested the business for too long. Starting today we are going to focus on innovation and growth!"

The team cheered and then got right down to work creating the innovation and growth plan. The plan included new products, improved quality, and a big investment in consumer marketing. Promotional spending and short-term sales incentives were cut.

Everything looked perfect until one very small detail became apparent. While the division manager believed passionately in growth and innovation, the CEO needed the division to continue delivering profits. The CEO also believed in growth and innovation, but not at the expense of short-term profitability.

When the division financial team actually started working on the numbers, it quickly became apparent that all the innovation was going to be very costly, and the only way to hit the profit target set by the CEO was to rein back the innovation and growth spending and focus on proven business-driving metrics, including promotional spending and sales incentives.

And so, gradually, the entire growth plan was taken apart, piece by piece. The general manager still earnestly proclaimed, "We will reinvigorate this business, focusing on the right levers, not just the easy levers." But everyone knew that the truth was different; the growth plan had been shelved in favor of a plan that would drive short-term profits.

The marketing plan had been built on mistaken profit expectations, so it was just a bit of wishful thinking with no chance of ever happening. It was a waste of time.

A marketing plan that is built on the wrong objectives isn't going to succeed. You have to have the right targets.

So the third step in the marketing plan development process is particularly important: clarifying the goals and objectives. Early on in the planning process you have to clarify what the business needs to achieve over the course of the planning period, be that one, two, or three years.

This makes perfect sense. The entire reason for writing a marketing plan is to figure out how best to achieve the organization's goals. As a result, clarifying the goals and objectives is an early step. Growing profit in a business by 50 percent, for example, requires a very different plan than growing profit by 2 percent. And there is little reason to start formulating a plan until you know which it is. Similarly, building brand equity requires a distinct set of initiatives; it is important to know if that is a goal well before you get into creating a plan. As Quill's Sergio Pereira advised, "Always start with the deliverables."

Confusion on goals can lead to a frustrating cycle, where a team creates a marketing plan that achieves a certain set of numbers, but then is sent back to create a plan that delivers a different set of numbers. This inefficient spinning can be avoided by being clear on the goals up front.

Managers should never *assume* they know what the goals are. This frequently leads to trouble. As John Gabarro and John Kotter wrote in their classic article, "Managing Your Boss," "The subordinate who passively assumes that he or she knows what the boss expects is in for trouble. Of course, some superiors will spell out their expectations very explicitly and in great detail. But most do not."[4]

Some argue that goals should be the *result* of the planning process, not the starting point, because a business can set appropriate goals only after completing the analysis, selecting the optimal strategic initiatives and tactics, and calculating the likely result. In other words, goals should be determined based on a "bottom-up" not "top-down" analysis.

This makes logical sense but ignores the fact that for most businesses, the goals are not up for discussion. In general, there are clear targets that a business needs to deliver. In a public company, for example, investors have expectations for profit results. This means that the starting point for the marketing plan is clear: deliver the financial targets. When creating a marketing plan, a manager might as well start with the already established objectives. They can be refined and clarified during the writing of the plan, but usually they're already floating around somewhere in the executive suite. As Adobe's Mark Delman observed, "Ultimately, for better or worse, shareholders have expectations, so the P&L has to drive." Marketing veteran Andy Whitman echoed the thought, stating, "The targets have to be upfront. If the company has given expectations to Wall Street, those are the expectations."

A bottom-up approach will rarely deliver the needed profit number. For a variety of reasons, managers have a strong incentive to set very low targets. As a result, going through the process of rolling up financials is often a waste of time. For Sergio Pereira, setting the objectives is a fundamental task of leadership: "Bottom-up never gets you to your number. Bottom-up is an abdication of responsibility."

Early in the process, the goals do not have to be set in stone. It doesn't really matter if the profit target is 2 percent or 2.5 percent or 3 percent; in all cases, the general goal is slow growth. Indeed, in some respects it is better if the goal is a bit loose; this provides more flexibility longer term. It does matter, however, if the goal is 2 percent or 34 percent or 90 percent.

STEP 4: ANALYSIS, ANALYSIS, ANALYSIS

Once a team has checked the foundation and clarified the goals and objectives, it is time to get to the analysis. This is an important step in the planning process; you can't create a good plan if you don't understand the business.

Ultimately, a business will succeed if it develops strategic initiatives that capitalize on the market trends and business strengths.

This requires a deep understanding of the situation. As one marketing veteran observed, "Without a good sense of the market, I don't know how you create a marketing plan. I don't believe you can move forward without understanding what has been happening."

Analyzing the market is a working step; this phase is all about serious study and thinking. It isn't about constructing presentation pages. The temptation to simply transfer data onto slides is enormous, but doing so won't help all that much. Creating pages without knowing the overall story and how the pages will be used does more harm than good.

The analysis step is a risky one, though the risk in this step isn't that the ideas will be flawed or the analysis weak. The risk is that the team will get lost in the data and spend months wading through information that is interesting but not particularly useful. There is much to analyze in any business; it is not hard to fill the time with interesting contemplation and reflection. The problem is that simply analyzing data doesn't add a lot of value.

The analysis supporting a marketing plan should not focus on the business basics. The basics are probably well known, and in any event they won't lead you to a bold new idea.

Instead, the analysis supporting a marketing plan should look at what is changing and what is new. What are the changes in the market that might present opportunities or risks? What are the consumer trends that might create opportunities for growth? Where are the financial risks?

There are many ways to analyze a market and many frameworks for a manager to apply, and a good number of these are very helpful. The key thing to remember is that the focus should always be on what is new and what is changing and how that creates opportunities. Two basic analyses to consider are the SWOT and the three Cs.

SWOT ANALYSIS

No discussion of marketing plans would be complete without a review of the famous SWOT analysis. It is one of the most com-

Exhibit 6.1   SWOT Analysis Framework

Strengths	Opportunities
Weaknesses	Threats

mon and well-known analytical techniques for understanding the situation facing a business.

A SWOT analysis is very simple. You take a paper and draw a two-by-two matrix. In one of the four boxes, you list the strengths the business can build on (S); in the other boxes, you list the weakness the business has to deal with (W), the opportunities presenting themselves in the market (O), and the threats on the horizon (T). On one page you then have a summary of the situation facing a business.

The power of a SWOT analysis is that it forces you to consider each of these important topics. It provides an easy, usable framework for studying a business. Trying to figure out exactly what is happening in a business is challenging. Identifying the components of a SWOT analysis, however, is straightforward.

A SWOT analysis is a useful tool, but like all tools, it has limitations. One of the biggest issues is that it doesn't really lead anywhere. The analysis provides a good overview of the issues facing a business. It doesn't, however, indicate what should be done. Connecting a SWOT analysis to strategic initiatives can be difficult.

THREE Cs

Another very helpful framework for analyzing a business is the three Cs analysis. This analysis focuses on understanding a business's customers, competitors, and channel partners. Analyzing each of these players is critical to understand the situation facing a business.

As in a SWOT analysis, the three Cs provide a simple and clear starting point for analysis. Unfortunately, just like a SWOT, the analysis doesn't lead logically to action; it is simply a solid and useful approach to build a deeper understanding of the business.

Customers are the people who ultimately buy and use your product or service. These are the people that matter most. Understanding the issues they face, their concerns, and their needs is a basic marketing step. It is impossible to succeed if you don't understand and delight your customers.

Competitors also play a critical role in market planning; anything a company attempts to do will be affected by the actions of competitors. Competitors are an unfortunate fact in the world of business; life would be much easier without them. In many ways, competition is the most challenging factor for business leaders; if there were no competition, business success would be fairly assured. Indeed, as Sergio Pereira observed, "Strategy is ultimately a competitive game."

Weak competitive analysis is a problem in many plans; the team comes up with a host of interesting strategies and tactics but neglects to consider the competition. Tropicana's John Bauer has seen the importance of competitive analysis. "Most marketers do not really understand how they stack up to competitors," he said. "They don't spend enough time understanding the competition."

Channel issues are important and frequently neglected. If a business doesn't form strong relationships with channel partners, such as retailers and distributors, it can be blocked from the market entirely. If your customers don't have access to a product because your channel partners don't carry it, your customers can't and won't buy.

The three Cs analysis is a useful way to analyze the challenges—as well as the opportunities—facing a business. Successful marketing plans are built on a deep understanding of all three key factors.

STEP 5: IDENTIFY STRATEGIC INITIATIVES AND TACTICS

Identifying strategic initiatives and tactics is the most important step in the planning process, the one that actually drives the value of the plan; in many ways the first four steps all build to this.

This is also the most difficult part of the planning process, because it entails narrowing your options. Given all the things you can do with the business, what will you focus on?

It is important to focus on strategic initiatives first. Selecting a particular tactic is difficult if you don't know what you are trying to achieve. A social media program, for example, might make good sense if you are trying to deepen your relationship with customers. It will make little sense if you are trying to reduce your costs.

Most businesses have dozens of potential strategic initiatives, and these initiatives almost always appear attractive. The challenge in this step of the planning process is to find the most compelling strategic initiatives to pursue and the best tactics to use to achieve each one.

This is hard work; the options are numerous, and making decisions can be difficult. Instinct might encourage you to choose many options, each one very broad, giving you the freedom to do almost anything. This is not an effective approach.

The question is really quite simple: In the big picture, what needs to happen to drive growth, and where will that growth come from?

Developing strategic initiatives is not easy. Sifting through reams of data, forming judgments about future trends, and then selecting the three or four best initiatives can be incredibly challenging. Starwood's Barry Sternlicht has observed that some people struggle with identifying strategies for a business. He explained, "Even with all the facts in front of them...some brilliant people still can't form good opinions because they can't figure out what the data in front of them means."[5]

THREE QUESTIONS

When thinking about strategic initiatives, it is useful to ask three simple questions about a business. These questions can help you identify the opportunities with a business and narrow down the focus.

Question 1: Grow Share or Grow the Category?

The sales of any business are a function of the size of the overall industry, or the category, and the market share of the company. Indeed, the following formula is always true:

Category Sales × Product Market Share = Product Sales

The size of the category times the market share for a particular product will always equal the sales of the product. This is always true; it is just math. If a category has unit sales of 2 million units, for example, and a particular business has a unit market share of 25 percent, then the sales of that business will be 500,000 units. Category times share will always equal sales.

As a result, if sales are going to go up, either share or category will have to increase in size. If the category is flat and market share is flat, then sales will be flat. If the category is growing and share is up, then sales will be up.

A marketer can then ask a rather simple question: What is the bigger opportunity for this business, increasing the size of the category or increasing our market share?

This may seem like a rather abstract question, but it is actually critically important because the tactics to build the category are very different from the tactics to increase market share. For example, financial services giant UBS could increase sales in its personal financial services business by building the overall category; it could tell people that having a professionally developed financial plan is important, and it could highlight the tax benefits of establishing a trust. UBS could also focus on building share; in this case, it could explain what makes UBS better than other financial services companies, or it might provide a discount to lure competitors' customers.

It is very difficult to build category and share at the same time because the tactics are different. Initiatives that build the category are all about increasing the size of the industry. Initiatives that increase share focus on building differentiation versus other competitors. An initiative that builds the category will generally do little to build share, and an initiative that builds share will do little to build the category. A manager has to choose.

Question 2: Penetration or Buying Rate?

Sales of a business are a function of how many customers the business has and how frequently they purchase.

Penetration measures the number of customers. Buying rate is the average number of purchases over a period of time, frequently one year. So the following formula is always true:

Penetration × Buying Rate = Sales

The number of customers (penetration) times the average rate of purchase among the customers (buying rate) will always equal sales.

The only way sales on a business will increase is if either penetration or buying rate is going up. If the number of customers remains constant (penetration) and the rate at which they purchase doesn't change (buying rate) then sales will not change.

So a manager should think about another very simple question: What is more important, increasing penetration or increasing buying rate?

As with growing category and increasing share, the tactics for increasing penetration are very different from the tactics for increasing buying rate. To increase penetration, a business has to go out and find new customers. This process will often involve broad marketing efforts and some very high-value incentives to get people in the door. To build buying rate, a business has to get current users buying more. This will frequently involve targeted marketing efforts, with incentives that reward loyalty or size of purchase.

A coupon in the Sunday newspaper is a marketing tactic that could be used to support growth in penetration or buying rate. But it would differ depending on what it was trying to achieve. To build penetration, the headline might say, "Try This Great Tasting Product!" and the coupon might be a high-value offer off of one item. To build buying rate, the headline might communicate a usage idea, such as "Try This New Recipe!" and the coupon would probably offer a low value off a multiple purchase.

As a result, thinking about penetration and buying rate is important.

Question 3: Awareness, Trial, or Repeat?

For any product to be adopted by a customer, three things must occur. First, the customer has to be made aware of the product. At a very basic level, the customer has to know the product exists. Second, the customer has to try it. Nothing will happen unless a customer actually tries the product. Third, the customer has to repeat, to come back after the trial experience and buy the product again. This progression is true for every product in the world.

Awareness → Trial → Repeat

So the third question to consider when creating strategic initiatives is this: Which is more important, awareness, trial, or repeat?

As with the other questions, the tactics for each of these things are different. Tactics that build awareness are different from tactics that build trial, and these are different from tactics that build repeat. It is impossible to do everything at the same time.

Being clear on the challenge is essential. If you don't know whether awareness is more or less important than repeat, it will be impossible to formulate a plan; the tactics that do one thing very well usually do another thing very poorly. A piece of mass market advertising, for example, is likely to be good at building awareness, but not at all effective at building repeat. A coupon printed on the inside of a package is a terrible awareness-building tactic but is probably quite effective for repeat.

PROFIT EQUATION

The goal of any for-profit business is to make money, and this is an important matter for many nonprofit ventures as well. When all is said and done, profit needs to go up. This is why profit is so often one of the goals in marketing plans. Profit is what matters most.

It is useful, then, to understand some basic finance. You don't need to know much about hedge funds and derivatives to create a marketing plan, but you do have to know a bit about finance and the way a business makes money.

On a very simple level, the profit of any company is simply the sum of profit from one business unit, plus the profit from the next business unit, plus the profit from the next business unit, less corporate overhead and the cost of capital.

Company Profit = (Profit from business 1 + Profit from business 2) – Overhead – Cost of Capital

So at Microsoft, for example, the company's profit is the profit from Windows plus the profit from Office minus the losses on pretty much every other business unit less corporate overhead such as CEO Steve Ballmer's salary and the company jet.

The profit on a particular business is always a function of the number of units the business sells, times the margin made on each unit, less the marketing expense involved to achieve those sales, less the direct overhead. In an equation, it looks like this:

Business Profit = (Units × Margin) – Marketing Expense – Overhead

As discussed above, unit sales on a business are always a function of the size of the market (category) times the portion of the market that goes to that company (share). Margin is always price less direct product costs (COGS). Marketing expense includes things such as advertising, promotions, and public relations efforts. Overhead includes the cost of the office space, R&D expense, salaries, benefits, and parties, among other things.

You can put all of this together into a simple formula that summarizes things in a very simple way. There are several components to the formula:

P = Business Unit Profit
C = Size of the Category
S = Market Share
OH = Overhead Expenses
M = Marketing Expense

Combined, the formula looks like this:

$$P = ((C \times S) \times (Price - COGS)) - M - OH$$

This equation is a useful tool for thinking about a business. If profit is going up, something in the equation must be working in favor of the business. The category must be growing, or market share must be increasing, or pricing must be going up, or some other factor must be working. There isn't anything else.

It is possible to analyze most businesses using this equation; by thinking through the parts, you can get a good understanding of the challenges facing a company. By looking at the trends affecting each part of the equation, it is fairly easy to see the profit picture facing a business.

The Gillette razor business is a good example of this. In the United States, the category trend is basically flat; the population is growing slowly, and most people shave. Gillette has a very high market share, and the market share is basically flat. The only brands of note left in the market are Schick, Bic, and store brand. Share isn't likely to go up much in the future. The cost of goods sold is small (plastic and metal) and probably flat; the cost of producing a razor is not substantial. Marketing expenses and overhead are both probably flat. The only lever that is increasing for Gillette is price, and this will remain the key lever. To grow profits, Gillette has to find a way to steadily increase prices. Historically, Gillette has done this by launching new products, each one more expensive than the last. Many years ago, Gillette launched Trac II. Later the company introduced Atra, then Sensor, then Sensor Excel, then Mach 3, then Mach 3 Turbo, then Mach 3 Power, then, most recently, Fusion. Will Gillette continue with this approach going forward? Given the profit equation and the importance of price, it is highly likely that there will be more new products in the future.

The profit equation is a wonderful tool for identifying strategic initiatives. When looking at the equation, it is useful to study each lever. Is reducing cost a big opportunity? Is building share? Is growing the category? Each of these questions can lead to a strategic initiative.

Remember, though, that a business can't do everything at the same time. It is impossible to grow the category, increase market share, raise prices, cut costs, optimize marketing spending, and reduce overhead all at the same time. Once again, you have to choose.

INITIATIVES TO TACTICS

Once the strategic initiatives are clear, you can then evaluate the tactics. These are the specific programs and activities that will ensure the success of the strategic initiative. Remember that you can't select tactics until the strategic initiatives are clear. Every tactic should be linked to an initiative.

The process, then, is first to identify the big initiatives and then think about tactics, or how the initiative will come to pass. The first step should always be identifying the initiatives; the second step should always be tactics.

Developing great tactics requires analytical rigor. You have to know the numbers behind the tactics to get a sense for what will work. This is where return on investment (ROI) should come up as a discussion point; what is the most efficient way to execute against the strategic initiative?

Great tactics also require creativity. Some of the best marketing programs are the most unexpected, simply because these tactics attract attention and generate excitement.

The challenge when formulating tactics is to think broadly about different ideas, and then use analytical rigor to select the most compelling options.

STEP 6: CHECK THE NUMBERS

By this point in the planning process, much of the plan is complete; the goals are set, the strategic initiatives are clear, and the tactics are penciled in. Things seem relatively set.

The next step, however, is also important. Before going any further, it is essential to check the numbers and look at the overall financial picture to be sure the plan holds together and the numbers work. This involves creating a rough profit and loss statement for the business, including rough estimates of sales, revenue, spending, and profitability. Only then will the marketing plan work. When the plan is quantified, the profits have to be achievable.

In many cases, this is where things become difficult. For most people, identifying things to do isn't all that hard; there are all sorts of good tactics to pursue. Making sure the figures work is much harder. As Adobe's Mark Delman observed, "It's one thing to say you want to grow 10 percent a year. It's another to really understand how you will get there."

The focus should be on developing a rough P&L that uses *reasonable* assumptions. Attempting to finalize every aspect of the financials is not a productive exercise; it requires too much time, and the financials take over the plan. Detailed financials should be created as part of the annual budgeting process, not the marketing planning process.

The key question in this section is whether the recommended initiatives and tactics will deliver the financial objectives. Will the plan succeed? If it's clear the plan won't deliver the profit goal, then the team must rethink the plan. It may be that the strategic initiatives are not appropriate given the financial expectations, or that the tactics are too costly. If the financials don't work, the team should go back several steps to complete more analysis and review the strategic initiatives and tactics.

Pushing forward with a marketing plan when the financials clearly don't work is a mistake; the plan will ultimately be doomed. The business either will miss the projections, which is an unpleasant proposition, or it will need to take additional steps to achieve the projections, in which case the team should have made these critical decisions during the planning process. As Dave Barger, CEO of JetBlue Airways, observed, "Hope isn't a plan. You better assume that plan B is not going to materialize, either, so what's plan C and D?"[6]

In some cases, achieving the financial projections for a business requires drastic and strategically foolish actions; the business might have to cut all its equity spending, or reduce product quality so much that it jeopardizes customer satisfaction, or take a price increase that will generate profit short term but create problems long term.

In this situation, the team should review the issue with senior management before creating a full marketing plan so as to determine the best course of action. Ideally, targets can come down to allow for a feasible plan. Worst case, if extreme action is necessary, then everyone understands that the plan will damage the business.

STEP 7: SELL THE PLAN

Before you can implement a marketing plan, you need to secure support from senior management and cross-functional groups. A brilliant plan that lacks the support of the organization is essentially useless; it will be impossible to execute it. The best strategic initiatives will do nothing if key cross-functional players don't support them.

As a result, selling the plan is a critical step in the process. Before you move forward, you have to be sure that the right people are on board. This step includes writing the actual marketing plan, presenting it to key people, and securing approval.

You can only work on this step after you have completed all the preceding steps. You must first have finished the analysis, identified the objectives and initiatives, and chosen the tactics. Indeed, starting to write a plan before the content is clear usually leads to a weak plan, full of pages that contain accurate data but don't point to achievable recommendations.

The process of writing and communicating a plan is not easy, and it is not quick. All too often teams spend so much time creating the plan and checking the numbers that they neglect to set aside enough time to do a good job writing the plan. This, of course, is an enormous mistake. At the end of the day, the plan must be written well; shortchanging this part of the process is an easy way to get into trouble.

When writing a marketing plan, the idea is to lay out the recommended goals or objectives, strategic initiatives, and tactics, and then explain precisely why they will work.

You then have to present the plan to key decision makers, both senior executives and cross-functional leaders. Gaining true support is essential; the goal is to ensure that people really believe in the ideas. Tepid support is a dangerous thing; you might walk away thinking the plan is a go but later discover that many questions remain. This is frustrating and inefficient. As Gary Ramey, senior vice president at Gold Toe Hosiery, observed, "You have to get everybody together. If everybody doesn't buy in, you have confusion."

Early in my career, a colleague advised me to be wary of those he called "the grinners." These are people who smile and say very pleasant things in a meeting, but who later vigorously attack the recommendations. He was right, of course. "The grinners" seem positive but end up being extremely destructive. If you encounter some of these people, it is best to spend extra time meeting with them to be sure you know where they stand and can address their issues.

Once senior management signs on to the plan, it is then important to communicate it to the extended business team. This includes all the people who work for a business on a regular basis. People have to know what the plan is to feel a part of the business, and leaders want their team to be fired up and engaged. The best way to do this is to be certain the team understands the plan and believes it will happen. This is particularly important at larger organizations. As Allen Questrom, CEO of JCPenney, explained, "The bigger the company, the more you have to sell the strategy to the organization. The more people who understand the strategy, the more likely it will get executed."[7]

The process of communicating with the extended team includes meeting to go through the plan, answering questions, and conveying excitement and enthusiasm. It involves telling people about the plan in multiple venues, including e-mail messages, business update meetings, and individual meetings. As Intel CEO Andy Grove observed, "When you have to reach large numbers of people, you can't possibly over-communicate and over-clarify."[8]

Keep two essential things in mind when communicating with the larger team. First, it is best to begin this task after senior management approves it. Taking the team through a bold plan before it has been approved can create a tough situation; you might have to explain why the exciting plan isn't going to happen. Don't get people fired up about a dynamic set of strategic initiatives and tactics until you are confident the plan will actually come to fruition.

At one point in my career, I was leading a team responsible for a small but promising brand. The team was passionate about the business and truly believed the brand could grow into a much larger business. I agreed. So, working with the team, I created a plan to jump-start the business with new products and new advertising. I then took the entire team through the complete plan. It was an impressive piece of work, and the team was excited about the potential of actually building the brand they loved so much.

Unfortunately, I wasn't able to sell the plan to senior management. There was an element of risk in the plan; it was not certain that the new products would work and that the advertising would have the intended impact. And, when all was said and done, I couldn't convince the division general manager to take a risk on a small business; he was willing to take risks, but he had to be selective about it, and other brands were taking some big risks at the same time.

This was a discouraging situation for the business team. The bold, exciting plan wasn't going to happen. Instead, senior management called on the group to prop things up and build profits with a set of small, tactical moves.

The lesson is that there is a time to tell the extended team about the marketing plan, and it is essential to do this. But that time comes after you are confident the plan is actually going to happen.

The other thing to keep in mind when communicating with the larger team is that the message should be positive. There are two ways to look at any plan. There is the pragmatic, somewhat cynical look that savvy, experienced executives often provide, with a focus on looking for the holes and the risks and the uncertainties. There is also the upbeat, positive, and excited look, with a focus on the big ideas and the potential.

When communicating a marketing plan to the broader team, it is best to take the upbeat, positive view; there is no reason to explain to the entire team why the plan might not work, and why the plan isn't really attainable, and why everything might collapse.

The goal when communicating with the team is to build understanding, commitment, and enthusiasm.

STEP 8: EXECUTE AND TRACK PROGRESS

A marketing plan is completely useless until it is executed. The best ideas written on paper will do nothing to build profits and sales until they are brought to life in the market. Execution is critical. As Procter & Gamble's A. G Lafley observed, "The only strategy anyone ever sees is what is executed in the market."

There is a long-standing debate in the business world about the relative importance of strategy and execution. Some people argue that strategy is more important because a bad strategy will fail regardless of the execution. If you execute a terrible strategy brilliantly, according to this argument, you will simply fail faster and in a bigger way. Other people argue that execution is more important because the best strategy in the world will not succeed if the execution is weak. A wonderful new product won't sell if it never gets on the shelf or if it isn't in stock when people want to try it. The truth, obviously enough, is that both strategy and execution are important.

A good marketing plan leads to good execution; people know what to do, senior management provides the needed resources, and the core direction is clear. This is how a great marketing plan drives a business; when all is said and done, a business with a strong plan has direction and focus, which leads to positive long-term results for the organization.

Many factors drive strong execution. Indeed, the topic of execution could fill a large book, and it has, many times over. There is far too much to explore in depth here.

However, two things are particularly important when it comes to linking marketing plans to execution. First, the next steps should be clear. For the plan to proceed, a marketing plan has to identify what needs to happen and when. Without some clear next steps, the plan might simply be filed away and ignored.

Second, there must be milestones to evaluate how well things are going. Ideally, each strategic initiative should have a set of metrics that give an indication of whether or not the initiative is coming to pass.

If a strategic initiative is building awareness on a new product, for example, it would be reasonable to have specific awareness goals. By the end of the first quarter, awareness should be at 25 percent, and by the end of the second quarter, awareness should be at 50 percent. If awareness is only at 15 percent at the end of the first quarter, then clearly something needs to be done to adjust course.

A good marketing plan makes it easy to manage the business. If the key milestones are clear, a leader can watch them to be sure things are proceeding and the business is on track. At business update meetings, the team can focus on four simple questions:

Where are we on implementation of the marketing plan?
How well is it working?
Has anything significant changed since the plan was created?
If so, what should we do now?

These four questions can drive implementation and execution for the team, and ensure that the plan is actually coming to fruition.

AROUND AND AROUND

In the ideal world, the marketing plan development process flows step by step in a sequential fashion. One step leads to the next, and this in turn leads to execution of the plan and strong business results. So the planning process is linear and orderly and direct (see Exhibit 6.2).

However, seeing marketing planning as a nice linear process, with a clear start and finish, is actually a bit misleading. Things are not quite this neat and simple. There are two reasons for this.

First, when creating a marketing plan, you may have to go back a step at certain times in the process. If you have trouble identifying strategic initiatives, for example, you will need to go back to the analysis step. If you find that the financials don't work, you may need to circle back to the objectives, to set a more achievable set of targets, or to analysis, to look afresh at the data and find other opportunities.

Very frequently, when trying to sell the plan you will discover that things don't hold together. It might be that the plan doesn't seem to flow, or the analysis seems insufficient to support your case, or senior management doesn't agree with your point of view. In any of

Exhibit 6.2   Ideal Marketing Plan Development Process

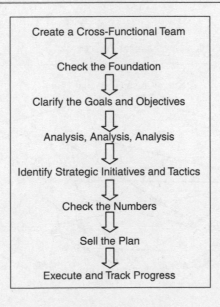

these cases, you need to step back, perhaps to think more about the strategic initiatives and tactics, perhaps to do more analysis, or perhaps to check the foundation once again (see Exhibit 6.3).

Creating a plan can be a frustrating undertaking in this respect; some days you think you are moving forward, but in reality you are moving back. Indeed, going back to do more analysis after you thought the plan was done can be discouraging. However, plans improve dramatically through this process; if there are holes in the plan, and there often are, it is better to find them and address them before the plan is executed.

Second, creating a marketing plan is not a one-time event; it is not a static process. The planning doesn't stop when execution begins. As soon as the plan is set and the team begins carrying out the tactics, it's time to start working on the next iteration of the plan, and the process begins again. As AspireUp's Roland Jacobs observed, "The planning cycle is a continuous loop."

If life were static, a business could develop a marketing plan and then rely on it for several years, at least until the strategies were all achieved and the tactics were brought to fruition. Unfortunately, that's not reality; life is constantly changing and evolving. As a result,

Exhibit 6.3   Typical Plan Development Process

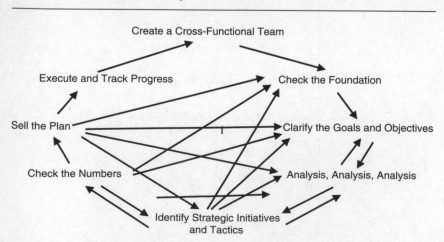

marketing plans are iterative documents; a business leader may revise marketing plans many times a year as situations change.

This is what keeps things challenging. Nestlé's Stephen Cunliffe stated, "Life never entirely goes as it is planned. There are always changes, and you have to adapt to them."

Any time the situation facing a business changes substantially, the marketing plan should be reviewed, because what was a good idea one day may no longer be a good idea the next. If a competitor launches a major new product, for example, the marketing plan may need to focus on defense. If product costs shoot up, pricing may become incredibly important, or cost reductions may suddenly become essential.

It is conceivable that a business team will need to create many marketing plans in a single year, each one modified based on the latest situation. Indeed, in a fast-moving industry, marketing plans will need to be updated and refined constantly. As Unilever's Andrew Gross noted, "As soon as you put together the document, it is out of date."

And indeed, the simple concept that life is always changing is perhaps one of the most forceful arguments in favor of creating simple, focused marketing plans. It is impossible to update a two-hundred-page plan frequently. It is very possible to update a ten-page plan.

In reality, marketing planning is a process that never ends.

*   *   *

It would be nice if you could simply sit down and, in a few hours, develop a marketing plan that would lead to guaranteed great results. Unfortunately, this is not the way things go. The best way to create a strong plan is to set aside enough time so that you can follow the important steps. Each step in the process plays an essential role, and skipping any of them can lead to trouble.

Chapter 7

WRITING THE PLAN

AFTER ALL THE ANALYSIS, DISCUSSION, and brainstorming, someone actually has to write a marketing plan. It doesn't just appear. Putting a marketing plan down on paper is a critical phase in the process. This step includes a bit of writing, a bit of strategy, a bit of analytical thinking, and a bit of showmanship. This is the place where everything comes together. It is in many ways the most important part of the process.

A marketing plan has to be written—and written well—to have an impact. If you don't write down the plan, you aren't likely to execute it. If you write an incoherent marketing plan, it generally won't work. This is true for three reasons.

First, until a plan is actually written down, it is simply a collection of ideas. Through the writing process, the plan takes shape and becomes real. Writing a plan creates commitment and clarity; it forces a manager to be precise about the recommendations. It is one thing to emphatically declare, "We need to invest in our brands and increase innovation!" or, "We should invest in advertising and public relations, and reduce spending on promotions." It is a very different thing to write down precisely what this entails and how the ideas fit into the overall plan. Investing in advertising and reducing promotions are lovely concepts, of course, but until the overall plan is created, the ideas are just that: ideas.

Second, and perhaps more important, the people who will see the plan don't see the interim steps. They don't see the process. They don't see the discussions, the analysis, or the debate. They only see the final written plan; they see the recommendations and the logic and the facts.

The people reviewing a plan really don't care about the work that went into creating it. The fact that a team spent weeks analyzing a market, or devoted three full days to debating alternatives, or constructed an elaborate multivariate regression to forecast the market size is completely irrelevant to the merits of the plan. Dutifully following the steps of a marketing planning process is good, but it is not a substitute for a strong recommendation. A team that carefully follows a process and produces a muddled marketing plan has achieved very little indeed.

The people reviewing a marketing plan simply see the plan. The written document is the output. This is true whether a plan is fully written out or is simply a presentation. If the plan is well constructed, it will make sense, and the decision makers likely will approve it. If it is hard to follow, your audience will question, challenge, and debate it—and rightly so. This is true for the senior executives, the people who ultimately will approve the plan. It is also true for the team that will execute the plan. In both cases, the written document has to hold together; it has to be credible and it has to be convincing.

Third, writing a plan is a valuable process because issues frequently appear only as the plan takes shape on paper. One marketing veteran observed, "People don't *really* make decisions until the information must get put down on paper. The process of writing the plan actually becomes the process of forcing and finalizing all the important decisions. No one makes a real decision until something's written down on paper and the decision is in danger of being disseminated widely by a certain deadline."

Major issues have a rather unfortunate way of surfacing as the plan is being written, when the excitement of the brainstorming session has dissipated and all that is left is the plan on the page. Ideas that seemed wonderful in the moment frequently seem questionable when written down, much as a piece of art purchased on a tropical vacation sometimes seems out of place and amateurish when unwrapped at home.

Sometimes it is only after you lay out all the priorities that you realize the cost of all the planned programs far exceeds the money available. The fact that a competitor is probably going to react to a sharp increase in promotion spending with a similar increase, thereby negating the volume impact, sometimes becomes clear only when the rationale for the increase is written down.

Obvious questions tend to come up when a plan is put down on paper. Won't competitors react? Didn't we try that last year? Where will we get the money? Will consumers really respond to that? Is that enough advertising to break through?

As a result, writing a great plan is essential. You have to create a document that communicates, persuades, resonates, and inspires.

The writing phase is where many marketing plans go off the track; the ideas might be solid, but the plan never takes shape on paper. Somehow the concepts get muddled when written down. This is a big issue. If the ideas are great but the actual written plan is disjointed, the overall impact of the entire planning process will be nil; the great ideas will be lost in the muddle of the plan.

For many people, writing can be a struggle. Most business executives spend their days running from one presentation to another, then to the airport and then another meeting, checking voice mails and e-mails as they go. The day is full of stimulation and demands and action. It is hard to carve out a big block of time to sit down and write a plan.

This is why many marketing executives leave the writing process until the last minute. Instead of writing the plan, they look, desperately, for other things to do: check e-mails, return phone calls, organize the desk, and go through the change drawer. As one of my colleagues explained, "I would rather pick up dog poop with my hand than sit down to write something."

Writing a marketing plan is particularly difficult because, by the time the writing process starts, the team is often frazzled, exhausted both mentally and physically from the analysis and plan development. Writing the plan is not usually a step anyone looks forward to.

Procrastination is a dangerous thing when it comes to creating a marketing plan, however, because marketing plans get much better when they're actually written down. In addition, the process of writing can take a long time, with multiple drafts and versions. Delaying simply reduces the time for refinement and improvement.

All too often the writing phase is left for the very end of the plan development process, when time is short and energy flagging. Only when the deadline approaches does anyone sit down to write the plan. This is not a wise approach; good plans take time and energy and effort.

TIMING

So when should you actually write the plan? You have to pick the right moment. Starting too late is a problem because you won't have time to create a strong plan or address the issues that will almost inevitably appear during the writing process. Starting too early is also a problem.

When it comes to writing a marketing plan, you can't actually begin until you're clear on the recommendation. You have to know what you think should be done on the business before you can write it down. You have to know the goals or objectives, the strategic initiatives and the tactics. Indeed, if you can't complete the GOST framework chart, you're not ready to write the plan. The classic admonition, "Never put off until tomorrow what you can do today," simply does not apply when it comes to marketing plans.

Some particularly energetic people will be tempted to start writing the plan early in the development process because it gives the impression of progress. If the goal is to create a written plan, the logic goes, then actually writing something is a good thing to do. After all, progress is progress. And as the word count increases and the pages multiply, it appears that the marketing plan is actually taking shape. This is encouraging for everyone involved.

Unfortunately, writing a marketing plan before you know the core ideas is a bad idea. The document might look substantial. But this would simply be an illusion, much like a Hollywood movie set where buildings look sturdy but are just fronts with nothing behind.

In some ways, writing without a recommendation does far more harm than good because in the absence of a specific plan, all you can write down are facts and ideas. This seems helpful, but it adds little because there is no overall story connecting all the points.

Starting the writing process too early is actually one main reason marketing plans become so bloated. Once pages exist, they tend to stay, filling up a plan with useless, distracting information. Studies into human behavior consistently show that people hate to give things up. Once people have something, they want to keep it. This is true, too, with material in a presentation; people hate to discard pages. This is another reason why so many marketing plans end up as long, convoluted documents that people ignore.

The other problem with writing a plan before the recommendation is clear is that it can distract you from the real task of figuring out what should be done. Laying out data is fairly easy. It is also, in a strange way, satisfying; it gives the impression of productivity. Identifying strategic initiatives and tactics and making sure the plan holds together is hard. As a result, people can lose focus on the bigger issues.

While at Kraft Foods, I had the opportunity to manage a number of summer interns. Each one had a big project they worked on during the summer. For example, an intern on Kraft BBQ sauce looked at opportunities to market to Hispanic consumers, and an intern on A.1. steak sauce determined how the brand should partner with meat packers. At the end of the internship, they presented their findings to a group of senior executives; this meeting played an important role in determining whether the interns would later receive a coveted offer to join the company as full-time employee.

I quickly learned that without clear guidance, interns fell into an obvious trap: they got lost first in the data and then in the writing process. At the start of the summer, they looked around for relevant information and discovered, in almost every case, a virtually unlimited trove of data and facts. Then they started gathering up this information, making copies, and printing documents. After six or seven weeks of this, the interns found themselves with a huge stack of data—but no recommendations. This led to a sense of panic, so the interns began creating a presentation, producing page after page of information. With a few days left in the summer, the interns discovered that they had a long, impressive collection of pages with absolutely no ideas and no recommendations. The time leading to the presentation was then a terrible, sleepless scramble as they made a desperate bid to identify something of interest from the mass of data.

Before starting to write a marketing plan, then, it is essential to be clear on the recommendation. What precisely is the plan? If the answer isn't clear, it isn't time to start writing; it is time to keep working on the core plan.

This is not to say that the plan has to be 100 percent locked before the writing process starts. Indeed, very often gaps in the plan become apparent as the writing goes forward; this forces the team to go back to an earlier step in the process and results in a better finished product. It is wise to leave time for this. Still, you can't start writing until you know the basic message.

Getting the recommendations fully agreed upon and finalized by the business team can be a tough job. A deadline will force the issue with the team; decisions sometimes only get made when they must finally be committed to paper.

A KEY QUESTION: WHO IS YOUR AUDIENCE?

Before you start writing your marketing plan, it is essential to think about your audience. Indeed, every marketing plan should be written with a specific person in mind. The objectives, strategic initiatives, and tactics won't change, but the layout of the specific document might.

Thinking about your audience is important because the better you know who you are dealing with, the more likely you can create a recommendation that will resonate. Just as it is foolish to start working on an advertising campaign until you know your target market, so too is it unwise to start writing a marketing plan before you know who will be reviewing it.

The goal for a manager isn't simply to survive the marketing plan presentation, though this is how some people seem to view the process. The goal is to get strong, committed support. If the presentation is to a senior executive, the goal is endorsement and resources. If the presentation is to a cross-functional team, the goal is enthusiasm and commitment.

To get support, you must think about your audience and write your plan in a way that will resonate and motivate. There are a number of important questions to answer about your audience before you start writing the plan.

HOW DO THEY LIKE TO COMMUNICATE?

This is a very basic question. Does your audience like to read plans or listen to presentations? Or do they just like to discuss? Most people have a preference. As legendary business strategist Peter Drucker observed, "Far too few people even know that there are readers and listeners and that people are rarely both."[1]

Giving a long, detailed, written plan to a person who likes presentations will not work particularly well; he or she might not read the plan at all. Similarly, giving a presentation to a person who likes to read and think about material isn't going to work; he or she may long for more information and detail and need time to think about and process the plan. Apple CEO Steve Jobs apparently hated PowerPoint presentations. He liked to look at prototypes, talk, and draw on a whiteboard. If you are presenting to someone like this, don't bring a presentation at all; you should bring props and be ready to just talk through the plan.

Understanding how your audience likes to communicate has some immediate practical implications because marketing plans can be presented in many different ways. A marketing plan can be a written document or a presented document, or just a discussion with props and visual aids. The preference of the audience should drive the format.

The amount of information and the amount of commentary will, of course, be driven by the format. If you are presenting, you don't need to write down every piece of the story; you can speak to these details in the presentation. If you're submitting a document, however, the written word is all you have, so you must pay close attention to the writing and include all the key facts in the written document.

In organizations that have a clear marketing plan process, it will often be readily apparent whether the plan should be a written document or a presentation. Nonetheless, it is still important to know the preferences of your audience; if you are creating a presentation for someone who likes to read, for example, you will have robust pages with more information. If the presentation is for someone who likes to listen, the presentation should have less information and rely heavily on the spoken word.

WHAT DO THEY KNOW?

You must consider how much the audience knows about the business before writing the plan. If your audience is very familiar with the situation, you can move quickly to the recommendations, building on what the audience already knows. If your audience has limited knowledge of the business, however, you will need more explanation.

People have to know a business fairly well to understand the marketing plan. For example, it is impossible to assess ideas for Blue Bonnet if you don't know that Blue Bonnet is a brand of mainstream margarine playing in an intensely competitive market with many fine but relatively undifferentiated brands. The category is driven by brutal price competition, with each brand fighting for share largely on the basis of low-price promotions. Since price is driven by product cost, finding ways to reduce the cost of raw materials is a top priority.

If you are presenting a plan to someone who has very little knowledge of a particular business, you should seriously consider holding a separate meeting before the marketing plan presentation to provide an overview of the category and the industry and to cover the basics of the business. Understanding the industry is critical for appreciating the marketing plan, but attempting to both introduce an industry and present a marketing plan at the same time makes no sense at all; it is simply too much material for people to absorb in one long meeting.

Indeed, one of the reasons marketing plans often end up as long, cumbersome documents is that people feel the need to review basic industry details while presenting the plan. This can't be done, or at least it can't be done well; one part or the other of the presentation inevitably will suffer.

WHAT ARE THEY WORRIED ABOUT?

The focus of marketing is on meeting customer needs. The most fundamental marketing lesson is that people don't buy things just because they are good quality and fairly priced. People buy things that meet a need. As a result, a basic marketing task is thinking about the needs of your customer.

Executives should think about marketing plans in a similar manner: The plan is the product; the decision maker is the customer. A critical question, then, is what are my customer's needs? More important, perhaps, is this question: What is my customer worried about? How will my product meet my customer's needs and address my customer's worries? The simple truth is this: A plan that responds to and meets the needs of the customer will be more likely to be well received than a plan that doesn't.

For example, if you are presenting to the CEO, and you know that she is feeling enormous pressure from the board of directors and impatient investors to deliver good financial results, then the marketing plan needs to address short-term profits clearly. This is not the time for a plan that focuses on the long-term potential of the brand. The issue on the table is short-term profitability. Similarly, if you are presenting to someone who believes in the power of innovation and growth, the plan should, of course, highlight innovation and growth.

The goal isn't just to present what your audience wants to hear. Some people attempt to do this, as if the entire marketing plan process were something of a game in which the manager attempts to figure out what the senior executive wants to hear and then says exactly that. This is a rather tempting approach because it is easy and popular. If you know that a senior executive wants to increase prices in a business, for example, then including a price increase in the plan will help the plan presentation go smoothly. Similarly, if you know that there is an interest in new products, then recommending new products seems like a logical approach. And recommending a change in advertising agencies will be viewed as a good idea by someone who wants to change advertising agencies.

Simply presenting what you think a senior executive wants to hear, however, is a bad approach. Most important, this is an abrogation of the duties of leadership; it turns the marketing plan into an elaborate ritual of "corporate think." It is no fun to present ideas you don't believe in, and this approach is not likely to be successful. It is the rare executive who can present a plan with conviction when they don't actually believe in it. And at the end of the day, the person presenting the plan is usually accountable for delivering it.

The goal is to present recommendations that are right for the business in a way that maximizes the odds that your recommendations will be approved. In this context, understanding the perspective of your audience is essential; it helps you communicate clearly and then position your ideas in a positive light.

WHAT ARE THEY THINKING?

Presenting a plan that your audience is expecting and will like is quite easy. Going through a plan with some controversial recommendations is a very different thing. As a result, it is important to think about your recommendations and consider how they will go over with your audience. Will the plan be received favorably? Or will it be questioned and challenged? Is the plan expected and safe? Or will it come as an unpleasant surprise?

Although it is impossible to know for certain how things will go, it is usually possible to get a good idea. One way to do this is to ask probing questions in advance. Simply talking about a business with a senior executive will provide great context; if the conversation focuses on all the wonderful things that are happening in the company, then you know there may be a low appetite for radical change. If the conversation focuses on all the company's problems, then you know there is a need for substantial and dramatic change.

If you are relatively confident that a plan will be well received, you can get to the recommendations very quickly; you are on safe ground. However, if you think your plan will be challenged, you will be better off building more slowly to the recommendations, explaining along the way why the obvious alternatives won't work. Jumping quickly to the recommendations might cause an immediate negative reaction; instead of listening fully to the plan, your audience will likely look for reasons to attack and reject the recommendations.

GET TO THE POINT

A good marketing plan should quickly address two key questions. First, what precisely are the recommendations? Second, why do they make sense?

All too often the actual recommendations are hard to find in the marketing plan; there is so much information, analysis, and detail swirling around the plan that it is very unclear what precisely is being recommended.

A marketing plan should immediately get to the point and present the goals, the strategic initiatives, and the tactics, generally in this order. The topics follow logically. Strategic initiatives can only be considered once the objectives are clear, and tactics can only be evaluated in light of the initiatives. As Quill's Sergio Pereira observed,

"If you don't agree on the objectives and the pillars, the rest of the discussion is useless."

There is much to be said for following the most basic of communication structures: tell your audience what you are going to tell them, tell them, and then tell them what you just told them. In other words, give a clear, concise overview of the plan, then outline the plan in detail, and then provide a clear and concise summary. A marketing plan that follows this structure is on the right track; the plan should start with an introduction highlighting the key themes, then go through the plan in more detail, and then circle back to reinforce the key themes.

Being explicit on the recommendations is essential. Equally important is having a clear rationale. Why will the plan work? This is where analysis, facts, and detail play an essential role. The marketer must construct a case explaining why the initiatives being recommended are the best possible choices for the business.

Your audience—the people reviewing and approving the plan—generally has a stake in the game; they want the plan to be successful, just as the manager does. In fact, the careers of the senior executives reviewing the plan usually depend on the marketing plan being successful. For this reason, your audience has a major incentive to study the plan with a critical eye, looking for shortcomings and better alternatives. As Dell's Kevin Rollins explained, "Occasionally our managers develop emotional connections to businesses that they really want to drive. But we make them prove the opportunity to us, and if we're not convinced, we don't move forward."[2]

Providing strong, balanced support is essential to selling the recommendations and building credibility in the organization. Most senior executives can see right through people who are just telling them what they want to hear. They want to see facts and be convinced. As Starwood's Barry Sternlicht observed,

> In order to build an organization, you have to be able to delegate, and in order to be able to delegate, you have to have confidence in the

people working for you. You have to know that they're thorough in their research, that they gather all the facts they need, that they tell the truth about what they've found, that they form sensible opinions based on the data they've collected, and that they grasp the differences between fact and speculation.[3]

A good marketing plan explains clearly why the recommendations make sense and why they are the best recommendations for a particular situation. Facts and analysis then back them up.

FIND THE STORY

People who write great marketing plans tell a story; they find a way to connect different pieces of information and create a coherent, logical, simple narrative flow that ties the entire situation together.

Stories are powerful communication vehicles; stories are how people remember and process ideas. People have trouble remembering collections of facts. As a result, a marketing plan that reads like a story becomes memorable.

Consider the follow description of a business situation: "Our market share in 2011 was 43.1 percent, up from 42.6 percent in 2010. Share was 42.2 percent in 2009. Our key competitor had marketing spending of $39.1 million in 2011, up from $25.7 million in 2010 and $25.3 million in 2009. We spent $24.9 million on marketing in 2009 and $25.1 million in both 2010 and 2011."

Now cover the previous paragraph with your hand. Can you recall the market share in 2010 without looking? Do you know if the business has been growing share or losing share? Probably not; it is difficult to remember a collection of scattered facts.

It is far easier to remember this description: "Our business is doing very well, gaining share every year despite the fact that our key competitor increased advertising spending by more than 50 percent from 2009 to 2011."

People remember stories, not facts. If you want your audience to retain what is happening, you have to tell a story. Finding the narrative flow for a business is critical; you have to identify and tell a story that summarizes and supports the plan. The story then becomes the framework around which the plan is built, much as a skeleton supports flesh and muscle in a body.

The ultimate challenge for someone writing a marketing plan is linking together all the analysis, data, information, and ideas in a seamless flow. The very best marketing plans seem obvious and simple. The data all fit together; the points all make sense, and the story leads you logically from one place to another. Great plans set up the situation and then gradually pull you along through the story.

A good story will summarize the entire plan in three or four easy-to-follow sentences. Most important, the story sticks in the mind. Facts and details then make the plan robust and complete. You need both things: a story that is simple and facts that support it.

A core story might look like this:

- The business is having a very good year with both profit and revenue up more than 10 percent.
- The strong results this year are due to the new products we launched in the first quarter.
- Our key challenge for the next year is to continue growing despite flat category trends and the lack of a big new product launch.
- To drive the business next year, we recommend focusing on three things: invest in year two support for new product, expand advertising on the base business, and reduce costs by increasing efficiency.

The entire business situation and marketing plan is summarized in four simple, easy-to-follow statements.

For this reason, the ability to create a story is a core management skill; great leaders are able to summarize a situation and lay out a plan of attack.

Identifying the story is a challenge. Although it seems simple enough, actually finding the narrative thread isn't easy. Usually a team will have to spend some time hunting for the proper flow. Finding the core story is powerful, though; once you have it, the story serves as a road map for the entire marketing plan.

To find the core story, it is useful to try to summarize the entire marketing plan in three sentences. This is often called an "elevator pitch," because it's what you would say if you only had a minute or so to get your story across to someone in an elevator ride between floors. You can create the summary points by simply writing three or four sentences. Alternatively, you can talk to someone and try to summarize everything in a short statement. You can involve a group in the process, too, by gathering them together in a room and trying to summarize everything in three sentences on a flip chart. Or you could ask all the members of the group to go off on their own and come up with their own three or four sentences; then they meet back up and compare their sentences. Whichever points they have con-sensus on are the ones that are probably the strongest.

Sometimes it takes a while to find the narrative flow; you have to keep trying different approaches until one emerges.

For example, you might start with something like this:

- Our business is struggling; sales, profits, and share are all down versus the prior year.
- Results are weak because raw material costs are up and com-petition is spending aggressively. In addition, our new product did not achieve its goals.
- To jump-start growth, we need to focus on attracting new cus-tomers through advertising and high-value promotions.
- Despite these activities, sales and profits will be down again next year. Share will be flat.

As you look at the summary, however, it is rather clear that the story doesn't work particularly well. How does the recommended plan address the issues? Why is a profit decline necessary? What hap-pened to the new product, anyway? The flow simply doesn't make sense. The points don't connect to each other.

When a story doesn't flow properly, it is usually due to one or two problems. Either the story doesn't follow logically from one idea to the next, or the key premises are not right. In either case, you need to go back and rework the story.

A story doesn't need to contain all the data. Indeed, this is basically impossible; the story simply provides the framework. In the story above, for example, it is worth considering the new product. Was that an important issue? Or was the new-product flop just something that happened but not a key driver? If so, there is no reason to include it in the core story. You shouldn't deny that it occurred, of course, but there is no reason to elevate it unless it plays a major role later in the plan. As they say in theater, if you introduce a gun in act 1, someone should be shot in act 2.

A revised version of the story above might go like this:

- Recent results have been disappointing because of aggressive moves by our competition; despite higher product costs, competitive spending is up.
- To be competitive in the market, we have to respond to these moves.
- Our recommended plan calls for increasing spending on both advertising and promotions to match the competitive moves.
- This will result in continued profit declines but a stabilization of market share.

This version of the plan is easier to follow; the points flow from one to the next, and there is a logical progression. The recommendation didn't change, and the financial information didn't change, but the overall story is now tighter and more compelling.

It is difficult to create a strong story unless you understand the business well and are confident in your recommendations. It is tempting to wonder, "But what if I just dropped out an important piece of information? What if I get a question about that? Will someone think I'm missing the main points?" In the case above, someone might start to worry, "I'm not discussing the new product. Won't that look bad? Don't I need to include that?"

Being confident enough to simplify a marketing plan is essential. As General Electric's Jack Welch observed, "Insecure managers create complexity. Frightened, nervous managers use thick, convoluted planning books and busy slides filled with everything they've known since childhood. Real leaders don't need clutter."[4]

Once the basic flow of a story is clear, you can move on to constructing the specific pages that will be in the plan. The core story sets the basic direction and functions as an outline.

In many cases, the story becomes the introduction, the agenda, the outline, and the summary. It is the glue that holds everything together.

It is critical to make sure the story comes through as the plan gets longer and more robust. Each page or piece of information should fit somehow into the story. If a piece of data doesn't fit, it shouldn't be in the plan. If you are nervous about dropping it, you can put it in the appendix. Remember, of course, that few people ever actually look at an appendix.

When writing a full plan, it is essential that the headlines (in a presentation) or main points (in a written document) flow from one to the next. One helpful technique is "backing out" of your document by scrolling through and writing down just the headlines. In the best case, the headlines flow seamlessly, each one building on the prior headline and leading to the next headline.

Storyboarding is a technique that can be used to lay out a plan and make sure each page flows from one to the next before you get too far into the production process. This is a process of laying out the specific pages in a presentation to test the overall flow of the story as told by the headlines. Importantly, the focus is simply on the headlines, not on the detailed analysis. The goal is to check that one page flows logically to the next and that there aren't any obvious gaps in the story.

To storyboard, take a sheet of paper and draw three vertical lines and three horizontal lines, creating a series of nine squares (see Exhibit 7.1).

Exhibit 7.1   Storyboard Template

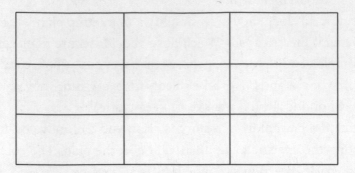

Then write a headline in each box, with a bit about what the page might eventually look like. If you think there will be a chart on a page, draw a rough picture of it. Each piece of paper, then, shows nine final pages in the presentation, so an eighteen-page presentation can be put onto just two pieces of paper. Don't include details; the goal is simply to see how the pages flow together.

It is best to do this in pencil; the power of storyboarding is the ability to go back and revise the headlines and the flow based on an assessment of how the story is working. Is support lacking for a particular point? Add another page. Are there obvious questions the audience will ask? Make sure they are addressed. Does a chart seem out of place? Change its location or drop it (see Exhibit 7.2).

The process of completing a storyboard forces a manager to be decisive; every page has to fit, every piece of data has to contribute to the story. When the storyboard is done, the entire plan should seem simple and easy to follow. Creating the final document is then quite easy; the storyboard is the map.

BE CONVINCING

Ultimately, the goal of a marketing plan is to gain support. In general, marketing plans are written down in order to secure approval or get buy-in. After reading or hearing a plan, your audience will ideally say, "Sure, this seems reasonable to me. Let's do it." And if things go

Exhibit 7.2 Storyboard Example

2012 is shaping up to be a terrific year. –sales up 10% –profit up 10%	The powerful results are being driven by our new product. –chart showing results	We believe we can continue to build our new product. –chart showing opportunity
Our goal for next year is to accelerate our momentum. –objective: +15% profit	Rising raw material costs will be a challenge. –costs are up by 8% –this has major impact	We recommend focusing on three strategic initiatives: –invest in new product –restructure trade promotion –reduce product costs
Our top priority is investing in year two support for our new product. –new product is doing well –we can invest further	To drive new product, we will maintain launch-year spending into year two.	We will focus activities on driving repeat business.

really well, you want to hear, "This is terrific. How can I help? What type of support do you need?"

For this to happen, a marketing plan must be convincing. The plan has to persuade people that it is the best possible solution. Considering the wide range of things a business can do, this is not always an easy task.

Once the story is clear in a plan, the task changes to providing the support points, or adding the data that backs up the recommendations. This is an important step in the process. A good story without support is just that: a good story. It won't persuade people on its own; you need data to prove your point and provide evidence.

This step can be time-consuming, as the relevant analyses and details must be written and inserted into the plan. If the story is clear, however, the process of adding the relevant data shouldn't be too time intensive. A few things are worth remembering during this step.

DATA, DATA, DATA

It is far more powerful to provide data proving a point than it is to simply state the point. An analysis that shows how margins have grown from 5 percent to 18 percent in five years is stronger than merely pointing out that margins have been increasing. Saying your competitor has been aggressive is fine, but presenting a chart illustrating how your competitor's advertising spending has gone from $52 million to $78 million in two years is convincing. Gary McCullough, CEO of Career Education, observed, "If you walk in and you've got the facts, you can usually carry the day."

Data loses much of its value and credibility without sources to back it up. Any important piece of information should come with a source. If you are making an estimate, state that. If it is a solid piece of data, note that. This increases the impact of data substantially. In addition, you may well be asked about the source for a piece of data; if you cannot remember it, which is likely, your methods will seem slipshod. According to advertising executive Stuart Baum, sources are essential. "You will be asked. And you will not recall. And this will make you look dumb and careless, or like you do not trust the source."

SIMPLIFY

The same sort of data can be presented many ways; you can write it, put it in a chart, or graph it. You can present a time series, showing changes over several years, or just look at a point in time. Using a fancy computer graphics program, you can put the data in a very elaborate chart.

The key is to find a way to present data that communicates clearly. The goal is for the data to be easily understood.

It is tempting to make information look complicated. A highly abstract, technical bit of analysis may seem impressive, but if your audience can't easily understand it, the analysis adds no value. Consider the following two statements:

Two plus two equals four.

We built a model based on a regression analysis of key business drivers that yielded an answer of four.

The first statement is simple, basic, and understandable. It's hard to lose people on the calculation. The second statement is complicated. It invites questions: How does the model work? What specific factors did you include in the regression? Without explaining exactly how the calculations work, the answer is simply a number. It requires a leap of faith; you have to believe the model to believe the number. The first calculation works much better.

On a rare occasion, you may encounter an analysis that is too complex to simplify. In this case, you have two choices. First, you could spend the time to explain it, going through precisely where the analysis came from and what it means. Second, you might decide that it is not worth the time necessary to go through the analysis in detail and simply not include the chart.

LESS IS MORE

Including less data is generally better than adding more data. It is better to have a few powerful reasons than a long collection.

Similarly, it is far better to space things out on several pages than to try to load everything onto one page. Filling a page with type and figures might reduce the size of your presentation or recommendation, but it does this at great expense; the document becomes almost unreadable. If you find yourself using tiny type to fit your points onto a page, you need to pare down the points or add another page.

REFINE AND REVISE

The final stage of writing a plan is refinement and revision. Your first draft will not be perfect. You must go back and improve it. Jim Kilts, former CEO of Nabisco, Kraft, and Gillette, would rewrite his marketing plans again and again. He explained, "It's not unusual for me to go through thirty, forty, or even fifty different versions and drafts before arriving at the final copy."[5]

It is important to leave time for revising because revisions will make the plan much stronger. It is also important to leave time for an outsider to read through the document. Often an objective observer can point out holes and issues in a plan that the team members can't see because they are too close to the subject matter.

During the revision process, it might become apparent that the plan simply doesn't hold together; the story doesn't work or the rationale isn't strong enough to support the recommendations. In this case, the team may have to go back and revisit the objectives, strategic initiatives, and tactics.

The revising phase is also a time to get input and buy-in from cross-functional team members. The best marketing plans come with the full support of the entire business team; the plan is endorsed by the cross-functional group. The sales team thinks it will work, the operations people have no concerns, the market research people are pleased the plan reflects their insights, and the finance people approve of the financial information included in the plan.

The easiest way to lose credibility in front of an executive is having a core team member introduce a concern or a major issue during the presentation. This instantly calls the entire plan into doubt, as executives begin to wonder whether the plan has been fully thought out and whether individual agendas are trumping the overall business plan. It also makes the presenter look unprepared, and it can be viewed as a sign of weak leadership. And, worst of all, it looks as if the team is hiding issues. This does enormous damage to the presenter's credibility and to the entire marketing plan.

As a result, a manager should involve the business team in writing and reviewing the plan. This is an art. A plan ultimately must have one primary author; otherwise it feels disjointed. However, the author must share ownership of the content to be certain that the team agrees and that the plan reflects the different concerns. Kraft's Greg Wozniak noted that he was able to both involve the team and create a coherent plan: "The business team owned it, but it was me writing it."

An important insight for managers is this: The best way to get team members on board with a plan is to let them review it and make comments and suggestions, and then address their input. Conversely, there is no easier way to create dissent on the team than to ask for comments and then not respond to the suggestions.

*   *   *

A marketing plan has to be written, and written well, to be effective. A great plan should quickly get to the point, tell a simple story, and be supported by facts.

Chapter 8

PRESENTING: THE BIG SHOW

THE MARKETING PLANNING PROCESS almost always comes down to a single, pivotal meeting, where the marketing manager stands up in front of a group of senior executives and, with her team, presents the marketing plan and answers questions. This is a critical moment.

If all goes well, the senior executives understand and support the plan. They are willing to provide resources and are enthusiastic about the future of the business. More important, they believe in the team that created the plan. The final approval may not come during the meeting itself, but it follows quickly enough.

If things don't go well, however, the outcome is much less positive; the executives don't follow or agree with the recommendations, and this leaves them with questions about the plan and the team.

It is sometimes painfully obvious when things go poorly; the audience drills the presenters with question after question, and the team struggles to respond coherently. Things can get rather ugly indeed. Once challenging questions come up, it can be difficult to keep the meeting on track. If things get very grim, the presenter may be forced to use his final lifeline, offering, "These are good issues. Why don't we regroup to discuss them later?" This, of course, means that the remainder of the meeting is largely a waste of time, much like a race being run under a yellow flag. The meeting finally ends with a resounding thud, as one of the senior decision makers concludes, "Well, I think we will have to talk more about this."

Sometimes, though, a weak plan meeting is more subtle; the executives nod and shuffle off. But they are unconvinced and shortly after the meeting begin raising questions.

The presentation, then, matters a great deal. The ideas are important, and the written plan is a critical document, but actually presenting well is essential; a great marketing plan poorly delivered will fall flat.

Creating a successful presentation seems straightforward: the team writes a good document and then someone gets up and delivers it. It isn't this simple, however; a great presentation requires thought and preparation. It doesn't just happen. Singer Annie Lennox explained it well in a recent interview, noting, "Preparation is everything. You need to rehearse so you're confident in the set, you know the songs very, very well and what's going to happen very, very well. It has to be flawless."[1]

NO SURPRISES

The most important thing for a manager to remember is that much of the work in selling a recommendation takes place *before* the presentation actually occurs. In almost every case, a team should know how the plan is likely to be received well before the presentation occurs. Similarly, the people listening to the plan should be familiar with the issues and know what sort of recommendations to expect. In an extreme case, everyone in the room may have already been through the presentation in advance of the meeting. This doesn't make the meeting a waste of time; it provides the forum to discuss the recommendations, uncover potential issues, and ensure that everyone is on board.

No one wants to be caught off guard when it comes to a marketing plan presentation. As Unilever's David Hirschler observed, "Your manager doesn't want a big surprise the day of the presentation." Similarly, the team working on a plan doesn't want a surprise; uncovering a major issue during the marketing plan presentation makes everyone look bad.

To avoid surprises, you should identify key influencers several weeks before the plan presentation. These people may be cross-functional leaders in the organization, members of the business team, or outside consultants and vendors. Advertising agency executives, for example, can be highly influential. You should then schedule individual or small group meetings with these key influencers to discuss the proposed recommendations well before the formal plan presentation to get input and secure support. If you aren't able to get buy-in, you should at least identify the issues. As Kraft's Greg Wozniak explained, "A lot of success is selling people on your ideas."

In addition to pre-selling to cross-functional teams, you should pre-sell to the senior executives themselves. This is particularly important if the recommendation isn't likely to be what they were hoping or expecting to see. The marketing presentation should never surprise people with bad news; this is not the time to announce that the business is performing poorly or that there is absolutely no chance of reaching the coming year's profit goal. This sort of news will dominate the discussion, cause concern, and make it extremely unlikely that the plan will be approved.

If you have successfully pre-sold a plan, you can be relatively confident about the meeting; it will probably go well. This is a good situation to be in, because you can then focus on making sure everyone agrees with the plan and you have access to the resources you will need to execute it.

SET THE STAGE

Any presentation is a show; it is a bit of theater. As a result, setting the stage is an important step. If the stage isn't right, the show won't go smoothly, and the audience will notice. The goal is to think about things well in advance and set them up thoughtfully.

GATHER THE RIGHT CROWD

You cannot have a great meeting if the right people are not there. For a marketing plan presentation, the key players have to be present. This will generally include senior executives and key cross-functional leaders.

You should think about your audience when considering who needs to be present. Some executives love large groups; they welcome the entire team and enjoy being the center of attention. There is an excitement and drama that comes with a full room, and they warm to this. For these people, large meetings work best; a crowded room is ideal. Indeed, these executives may actually be uncomfortable in a small group.

Other executives prefer small groups and are uncomfortable in larger meetings. If there are many people in the room, they might not ask questions and discuss issues. For people like this, it is best to have a very small meeting, with just a few people, perhaps five or six people in all. A large meeting would be unproductive because issues wouldn't surface.

At one point in my career I reported to a general manager who was extremely uncomfortable with large groups; I quickly learned that the best way to take him through a marketing plan was to simply sit down in his office and flip through it, one on one.

PREPARE THE ROOM

People make judgments quickly. The moment they walk into the conference room for your meeting, they are forming opinions about your plan and your team. If the group is scrambling to get ready, your audience might conclude that the team isn't prepared. If there aren't enough chairs, they might decide the group doesn't plan well.

It is important to prepare a room before any meeting, and especially before a marketing plan presentation. You don't want to learn that the projector doesn't work two minutes before you are supposed to start; it looks sloppy. Your goal is to set the stage for the plan presentation, to think ahead and make sure the obvious details are covered. This communicates that you and your team are thoughtful, organized, and ready.

The first step in preparing the presentation room is to make sure everything is technically functional. This seems obvious, but all too often the computer doesn't work, or the hookup to the projector fails, or the bulb in the overhead projector is out. How many times have you sat through a meeting where the presenter clicks futilely away at the screen with his clicker, only to have the projector fail to cooperate? You don't want that to happen to you at this critical juncture in the marketing plan process.

Other small details are equally important. Are there enough chairs? Is the temperature right? These details might not seem to warrant the attention of a marketing manager, but your audience will take cues from everything around them during the presentation. The old adage holds true: You never get a second chance to make a first impression. A presenter who struggles to get the projector working or who isn't ready at the designated time looks disorganized, and this hurts overall credibility.

ARRANGE THE SEATING

You want to get the right people in the right seats. The top executives, the one or two people who ultimately pass judgment on the plan, should occupy the most prominent seats. It's a good idea to put these executives wherever they will be most comfortable and surround them with people they trust. If the key decision makers feel secure, they may be more likely to support your plan.

SHOW CONFIDENCE

The attitude of the presenter is perhaps the most important element of a marketing plan presentation. Senior executives *need* to see someone presenting the plan with confidence, certain that it is the correct approach. Someone who is nervous and insecure makes everyone feel uncomfortable, and this makes the plan seem weak.

Senior executives usually analyze two things in a marketing plan presentation. First, they look at the plan itself. Will it work? Are there any major flaws? Then they look at the team and the team leader, wondering whether they can trust the recommendations and analysis. According to one marketing executive, senior managers ask, "How good a person is this? Does he know what's really going on? And what is he going to do about it?"

The challenge is to be confident without being too confident. As *Advertising Age* columnist Bob Garfield observed, "Think about the advice they give roofers and iron workers. You've got to feel comfortable up there, or else you'll fall. But you can't feel too comfortable, or else you'll forget where you are...and fall."[2]

Confidence comes from three places: practice, knowing the business, and having a firm grasp of the facts.

PRACTICE

Presenting a marketing plan is much like telling a story; you usually get better the more you do it. As Herminia Ibarra and Kent Lineback wrote in the *Harvard Business Review*, "Any veteran storyteller will agree that there's no substitute for practicing in front of a live audience. Tell and retell your story; rework it like a draft of an epic novel until the 'right' version emerges."[3]

The best way to become confident presenting a marketing plan is to practice. Assemble test audiences and present it again and again. Encourage people to ask tough questions. Listen for points of confusion. Watch their reaction. Do they nod their heads and follow the flow? Or do they look puzzled and start flipping between pages? Do they zone out and pull out their smart phones? The more times you do something successfully, the more confident you will become.

When you practice a presentation, you will learn one of two things: that the presentation works or that it doesn't. Either way, this learning is important.

A practice session might surface issues, places where the presentation doesn't quite work. This is a good thing because you want to identify the problems before the actual event. You can then take steps to improve the presentation, revising the flow, adding information, or clarifying the pages.

Sometimes you'll learn that the presentation works well. People follow it and see the logic. They understand your recommendations and why they will work. This is a positive outcome, too, because now you can be more confident. When you know something will go well, it is easy to project confidence.

KNOW THE BUSINESS

The most powerful way to project confidence is to really understand the business and the recommendations. If you are 100 percent certain you know the business and you believe fully that your recommendations are sound, then confidence will naturally follow.

To some extent, confidence is the natural result of a good planning process. If you've analyzed a business in depth, studied your customers and competitors, created a strong plan with powerful strategic initiatives and tactics, and checked the financials, it is easy to be confident.

FIND THE FACTS

Nothing creates confidence more than a few relevant facts. Opinion and subjective observation are dangerous territory; in the end, a question of opinion is usually decided by seniority or forcefulness. A presenter can't count on either. Facts, however, can be rock-solid bits of truth that hammer home a point without question.

So a great way to build confidence is to know the facts. When pressed, if you have solid pieces of data to drop back on, you'll be well covered. If a senior executive offers an opinion and you're able to counter it with a fact, then you should carry the day. A senior person can't just wish the fact away.

When using facts in a presentation, it is critical to understand exactly where they come from. If you say, "Thirty-seven percent of our customers in the industrial lubricants business want environmentally friendly products," you have to know the source. When someone asks you where you found the figure, you can't say, "Well, I have no idea," or, "I read it in some report," or reference a study from a market research firm that executives don't respect.

A manager who can't explain the figures looks self-conscious and confused. This is almost the opposite of confidence. Not knowing the source is a sign that the analysis isn't complete. As Daniel Okrent, public editor at the *New York Times*, wrote in a recent piece, "Number fumbling arises, I believe, not from mendacity but from laziness, carelessness or lack of comprehension."[4]

Importantly, you don't have to know *all* the facts, and you shouldn't even try to. It is impossible to know everything. Attempting to do so will likely cause confusion and a cluttered mind—not the mind-set you want on the day of a key presentation.

You just have to know a few critical figures that support key points in the presentation. Facts like this provide points of refuge when questions arise. They also send a strong impression to the audience.

Consider, for example, what happens when a presenter is questioned about the price sensitivity of the business, and she states without pause, "This business just isn't that price sensitive. More than 62 percent of our customers believe that our products are worth paying a premium for and our price elasticity is negative 0.71, well below the industry average of negative 1.06." The presenter will likely carry the point; there are strong facts that support the argument. More importantly, the presenter is sending a clear message: "I know this business inside and out."

When preparing for a presentation, it is useful to identify five, six, or seven key facts. These should be precise and unquestionable; you should know where each one comes from and the calculations behind the figure. You don't have to memorize the numbers; you can just write them on a piece of paper and lay it on the table in front of you. During the meeting, you can use the facts while presenting or, even better, casually drop them in while answering a question.

GET SOME ALTITUDE

Great presenters follow what I call the altitude principle. It goes like this: It is far better to encounter turbulence when you have lots of altitude than when you are flying close to the ground.

An airplane flying along at 35,000 feet can encounter a lot of bumps and continue safely on its way; it can drop 5,000 or even 10,000 feet and still be high above the ground. In extreme cases, people may be thrown about and injured, but the plane usually survives and reaches its destination. When an airplane is taking off or about to land, however, turbulence is a much bigger deal. At 200 feet, a plane that drops just 201 feet due to turbulence will crash and burn. This is unfortunate but true. It is partly why most airplane crashes occur during takeoff and landing.

This theory is useful when thinking about presentations, too. It is far better to encounter turbulence in the middle of a presentation than at the beginning or the end. If there is something in your materials that you think will be controversial, it's best to put it in the middle.

At the start of a presentation, the team is settling in and your audience is becoming familiar with the issues. This is the takeoff phase; it is the time to present well-known, established, and safe material. Your goal is to get people nodding and create a sense of alignment. Once you have some momentum, some altitude, you can move on to the controversial material. At this point, a bit of turbulence in the form of questions and debate is not a bad thing. Near the end of the presentation, as you enter the landing phase, it is again time to minimize turbulence; you don't want to finish with questions and send people off with doubts.

BRING IT TO LIFE

The goal in a marketing plan presentation is to secure enthusiastic support. To do this, you have to win both heart and head. Presenting a credible, solid plan that rationally makes sense is good but not sufficient; it might win over the head, but it won't win the heart.

To win the heart, you have to create excitement and enthusiasm. To really sell a plan and mobilize an organization, you must win the rational argument and the emotional argument. Great pages and a well-structured presentation can leverage the data, but the presentation must also exude flair and energy. As Bill Gates explained in his 2007 commencement address at Harvard University, "You can't get people excited unless you can help them see and feel the impact."[5]

Marketing plan presentations always benefit from props and show-and-tell. Simply explaining what you want to do is ineffective compared to actually showing what you want to do. Plans also benefit from the use of a theme or slogan; this makes the plan catchy and memorable. One marketing executive wrote a plan about a business turnaround and called it "The Year of the Phoenix." As marketing veteran Roland Jacobs observed, "You've got to have something to make it memorable. It's a silly little thing, but it makes a difference." Another executive gave four toy cars to each person in the audience—a Hummer, a Mini Cooper, a minivan, and a sedan—to make the point that customers have very different motivations, and trying to reach everyone at the same time would never work.

* * *

There is something very powerful about seeing a team stand up and confidently present a well-thought-out marketing plan. Done well, a plan presentation creates excitement and energy. This only occurs, however, with thoughtful planning, preparation, and practice.

Chapter 9
TWENTY STRATEGIC INITIATIVES

AT THE HEART OF ANY MARKETING PLAN lies the strategic initiatives; these are the big moves. This is the part of a marketing plan that really matters; it should be the focus of the discussion and debate.

Unfortunately, many people struggle to create tight strategic initiatives; they confuse strategic initiatives with objectives or tactics or values. This leads to a muddled plan.

The most important thing to remember is that objectives are what you hope to achieve with the business. Strategic initiatives are what you will do to achieve the objective.

This chapter presents twenty strategic initiatives. Not every one of these initiatives is appropriate for every business. More important, perhaps, is to remember that no business in the world could pursue all twenty initiatives at the same time. The goal of this chapter is to provide examples of strategic initiatives and spark your thinking about your own.

1. BUILD AWARENESS

If customers don't know about your product, they won't buy it. This is the basic reason why people worry about awareness so much and why building it shows up in so many marketing plans. Building awareness is a core marketing task.

Brand awareness on its own is not helpful; people can be aware of a brand and have no interest in buying it. Awareness without purchase intent is not a good thing. As one of my colleagues at Kellogg points out, she could take off her clothes and go running through campus naked, and this would create a lot of awareness. She also notes that the move might not create a lot of positive interest.

TACTICS

The most common way to build awareness is advertising; broad-reach media vehicles such as television and print ads can have an enormous impact. When a broad-reach advertising campaign kicks in on a new product, awareness will almost always shoot up.

Advertising isn't the only way to build awareness, though; literally hundreds of tactics will have an impact, from banner ads to billboards to blog posts. Indeed, anything that gets your product in front of people will contribute to awareness at least to a minor degree.

MEASUREMENT

For most businesses, awareness is fairly simple to measure. Questions such as, "What brands of potato chip can you think of?" can evaluate unaided brand awareness, and questions such as, "Are you aware of Wise Potato Chips?" can track aided awareness. Unaided awareness is more valuable and harder to build.

2. EXPAND DISTRIBUTION

People won't buy a product if they can't find it. A product that is not in distribution has no hope of generating sales. A basic marketing task, then, is to ensure that a product or service is present in key outlets. For some products, this means ensuring that stores carry the product. For other products, expanding distribution means increasing the number of distributors that stock the item.

Expanding distribution on its own will not guarantee success; demand must be present to drive sales. Indeed, distribution without demand is a dangerous combination; a retailer won't carry a product for very long if there isn't demand for it, as retailers only make money by selling things. As a result, distribution needs to be paired with other marketing initiatives to ensure that demand is in place to drive sales once distribution increases.

TACTICS

There are two important tactics to consider when expanding distribution. The first is offering incentives; a strong incentive can be a powerful driver of distribution. Offering a 35 percent discount to retailers who start carrying a product, for example, may be enough to get store owners interested.

The second tactic to consider is expanding the sales force. Adding salespeople means more people calling on channel partners, and more sales calls should eventually result in more distribution.

It is useful to think of distributors and retailers as customers, and then market to them just as you would market to end consumers; you need to understand your channel partners just as you understand your end consumers and select marketing tactics with the same amount of care. The better you know your channel partners and what motivates them, the more likely you are to create a compelling offer and achieve your goals.

MEASUREMENT

Distribution is easy to measure in most industries; you can simply track how many retailers or distributors carry your product and how many items each one has.

Distribution and high-quality distribution are distinctly different. A retailer that carries just one item from a twenty-item line has distribution, but the quality is low. As a result, marketers should watch absolute distribution (such as the percentage of retailers in a market carrying at least one item) and quality of distribution (such as average number of items carried).

3. BUILD BUYING RATE

Buying rate measures how much a customer purchases in a given period of time. Often a company will look at an annual figure, the number of purchases a customer has made in the past twelve months. Buying rate is a critical business metric because total sales of a product or service are always the number of customers multiplied by the buying rate, or average rate of purchase. This is always true; it is just math. Increasing buying rate, then, is one important way to build a business.

Building buying rate is particularly compelling because it involves selling to your existing customers, who are generally easy to reach and are already favorably inclined to your brand.

TACTICS

Buying rate tactics should spark more frequent purchases of products. One way to do this is through incentives such as frequent-flyer programs, frequent-buyer cards, and bulk purchase discounts; these offers reward larger and more frequent purchases with greater incentives.

Other buying rate tactics include reminder advertising, product quality improvements, social media campaigns, and loyalty programs. The more you engage with your customers and make them feel connected to the brand, the more you can build buying rate.

An increase in buying rate can come from an increase in total category purchasing or from an increase in loyalty. These are quite different: increasing the category involves selling the overall category benefit and driving use of the entire category; increasing loyalty is changing the mix of products purchased in a category from one brand to another.

MEASUREMENT

You can measure buying rate in several ways. In the best-case scenario, a company has data on each customer; with this data it is possible to track purchase rate by person or customer over time. A credit card company, for example, can monitor monthly purchases to get an immediate read on buying rate at a customer level.

Also, by surveying customers regarding how frequently they are buying the product, it is possible to evaluate buying rate. This approach is not as accurate as customer-level purchase information, but for some products it is the only information available.

4. BUILD PENETRATION

Penetration measures how many customers a brand has. As the sales of a product in a given period are always the number of customers multiplied by the buying rate, increasing customers, or building penetration, is an important and common strategic initiative. This is especially true for new or small brands with a limited customer base.

Every product in the world needs new customers. An existing customer base will always gradually erode as people move to new cities, companies merge and fold, and needs change. As a result, whether new or established, at some point a product has to think about attracting new people to the franchise.

TACTICS

Several things must happen to build penetration: people have to be aware of the product, have access to the product, be interested in buying the product, and be motivated to do so. Each of these steps can be a strategic initiative on its own, or the basis for tactical decisions.

Penetration tactics might include broad advertising to build awareness, or they might include sampling programs to drive trial, or high-value incentives to spark purchase from new customers. Indeed, anything that helps convert a nonuser into a user can be considered a penetration tactic.

MEASUREMENT

Penetration can be measured as an absolute number or as a percentage of customers in a market. Both are valid ways to look at penetration, but they do different things. Measuring the absolute number makes it easy to link penetration to sales. However, measuring absolute numbers ignores industry trends; increasing customers by 5 percent is good but not a great accomplishment if the number of customers in the industry increased by 25 percent in the same period. Measuring penetration as a percentage shows relative standing, or the portion of customers in a category who buy your brand. This approach shows progress versus the competition, but it isn't directly linked to sales; in a declining category, it would be possible to increase percent penetration while the absolute number of customers declines.

One challenge in measuring penetration is that the number of customers a brand has is constantly shifting; things never stand still. Penetration is driven by two factors: the number of new customers and the number of lost customers. If many people are giving up on a brand, the number of new customers could be substantial, but the total number of customers may not increase. As a result, the very best approach is to measure total penetration, the number of new customers, and the number of lost customers.

5. BUILD EXTENDED USAGE

One way to increase buying rate is to increase extended usage. This involves getting customers to do new things with a particular product. For example, people now use Arm & Hammer baking soda in all sorts of different ways; they put a box in the freezer, brush their teeth with it, and my personal favorite, pour it down the drain. This is good for the brand, as the core use of baking soda—baking—is declining quickly in the U.S. market.

Building extended usage is appealing; it is highly incremental and not likely to prompt a competitive battle. The challenge is that it can be very difficult to do because it involves changing the way people think about a brand. When I was on Miracle Whip, we spent a lot of time trying to get Miracle Whip consumers to use the product to make chocolate cakes and stir-fry chicken. This was a difficult task because most people only used Miracle Whip on sandwiches. Extended usage campaigns can also cause confusion; encouraging people to use margarine to moisturize their hair may lead people to wonder if the product is really food or a beauty product. Promoting this idea could actually hurt the base business; most people don't eat beauty products.

TACTICS

Building extended use is much like launching a new product. The only difference is that the focus is on an idea instead of a specific product. For a new use to take hold, people have to know about the idea (awareness), be motivated to try it (trial), and then try it again (repeat).

Each of these steps requires different tactics; advertising builds awareness, for example, but is not great for driving repeat purchases. Sampling programs drive trial but are ineffective at building awareness due to their small scale.

MEASUREMENT

Extended usage ideas can be measured like any other new product; it is possible to track awareness, trial, and repeat. The best way to gather this data is to use surveys, asking customers about the idea. Awareness evaluates how many people have heard of the idea, on either an aided or unaided basis. Trial looks at how many people have actually tried the idea. Repeat measures the number of people who have come back to try it again.

6. INCREASE LOYALTY

One way to drive sales is to increase loyalty with existing customers. Ideally, a brand has customers who are highly loyal, devoting all their purchases in a category to the brand.

Loyalty-building efforts focus on ensuring that customers don't use competitive products. For example, a consulting firm might encourage a current client to use the firm for all of its projects.

TACTICS

Loyalty can be built in many different ways. The key, of course, is that all efforts are aimed squarely at current consumers, the people buying the product today.

The most common loyalty efforts are incentives or promotions that reward increased loyalty. This includes "buy two, get one free" deals and frequent-buyer cards. These incentives can be very powerful; giving customers an incentive to buy a brand they are already buying will usually result in incremental sales. The problem is that these incentives can encourage customers to wait for discounts to purchase a product. More important, incentives can erode quality perceptions.

Loyalty efforts can also include tactics such as focused advertising, relationship-building programs, and product improvements. For business-to-business companies, tactics in this area might include relationship-building and volume discounts.

MEASUREMENT

One way to quantitatively measure loyalty is share of requirements. This calculation is simply a customer's purchases from a particular company divided by the same customer's purchases of the entire category. If a particular company does eight consulting projects a year, and two of them are with Accenture, then Accenture has a share of requirements of 25 percent. Increasing loyalty should translate into an increase in share of requirements.

The data behind share of requirements is readily available in some categories. For example, it is very easy to obtain this information for many consumer products. Similarly, in the commercial airplane market, loyalty information is well known across the industry; there is no question which airlines are flying which planes. In other categories, it can be difficult to obtain loyalty information, forcing a company to rely on surveys to measure.

7. STRENGTHEN IN-STORE MERCHANDISING

Anyone managing a product sold in a retail environment has to worry about the amount of in-store support that product receives. It doesn't take a PhD in marketing to realize that if customers can't find a product in the store, they won't buy it, or that a product stacked in the front of a store will sell a lot more than a product that can be found only on a high shelf at the back of the store.

Having a product in distribution is different from getting good in-store merchandising. Distribution involves establishing an initial presence. Good support involves securing a prominent place on the shelf and then getting an eye-catching position in store promotional activities.

TACTICS

A strong sales organization is usually essential to getting good in-store support; for most products, having people visiting stores will help enormously because these people can put up signs and stack up the product. Frito-Lay, for example, has salespeople visiting retailers almost every day, replenishing product and making sure that the Frito-Lay items are displayed prominently.

A number of other tactics can also help with in-store merchandising, such as developing collateral materials (signs and display units) and giving retailers financial incentives.

MEASUREMENT

In-store merchandising can be easy to measure by tracking the absolute level of activity in the store. For example, it is possible to look at the number of products on the shelf, the number of secondary displays in the store, and the amount of signage.

In some categories, this information is readily available from market research firms. This makes getting and tracking the data a simple process. In other categories, this information can be harder to assemble, forcing managers to rely on reports from the sales force or commission a special study.

8. IMPROVE PRODUCT QUALITY

A very simple way to drive better business results is to improve the product. A superior product will lead to happier customers, and happier customers will lead to increased sales and profits. This might come from increased loyalty, or it might come from increased use of the category in total.

The challenge in improving quality, of course, is that it generally increases product cost; quality is rarely free. This additional cost needs to be offset somewhere else in the P&L to avoid a drop in profits.

Ultimately, better product quality should result in higher sales, but this link is frequently hard to see. For a quality improvement to translate into more sales, customers have to notice the better quality and then change purchasing patterns as a result. This can take time. Telling people the product is now "new and improved" can actually cause a sales decline because the people using a product probably already like it, and they might not see the new version as an improvement.

TACTICS

In most cases, quality can be improved in obvious ways. Reducing defects, improving reliability, adding features, and enhancing customer service are all potential approaches.

The challenge, of course, is figuring out which quality improvements are most valued by customers; it is impossible to do everything, so a manager must choose which aspect to focus on. Market research can help with this, but only to a certain degree.

Any change in the product or service experience needs to reflect the brand. Improving style is not necessarily better for a brand built on tradition. Strengthening health benefits is not always a good thing for a brand grounded in indulgence. Enhancing taste can be a bad thing if a brand is all about consistency, as Coca-Cola learned in the 1980s with its introduction of New Coke.

MEASUREMENT

Quality is fairly easy to measure. In fact, the challenge in measuring quality is not finding something to measure, it is figuring out which metrics are most relevant.

The options are many. A company can track defects, product returns, and customer complaints. A company can also evaluate general customer satisfaction over time in a variety of ways.

The most important thing when it comes to quality is to measure something consistently to see how the measure changes over time.

9. DECREASE PRODUCT COSTS

A powerful way to drive profits is to reduce product costs. A reduction in costs will result in a direct increase in profits, assuming sales remain relatively constant. The challenge is simply to find opportunities to reduce costs while maintaining overall customer satisfaction, or to find opportunities where the financial benefit of a cost reduction outweighs the volume impact.

TACTICS

There are dozens of ways to reduce costs on a business. A company can increase line efficiency, utilize cheaper materials, negotiate lower prices on key raw materials, reformulate to cut product costs, or eliminate expensive and unnecessary features.

The challenge is to ensure that the cost-saving moves do not reduce sales or hurt the brand. This can be hard to determine; will customers notice if the label has two colors instead of three? Will anyone care if the product comes in thinner packaging?

There is a great temptation to pursue cost-saving opportunities— but these can end up hurting product quality and customer satisfaction. The benefits of reducing costs are immediate, certain, and quantifiable. The costs of such a move—decreased brand equity and ultimately lower sales—are in the future, uncertain, and hard to quantify. As a result, smart people can make very poor decisions when it comes to cost-saving projects, reducing quality despite the obvious risk.

MEASUREMENT

Measuring cost-saving initiatives is fairly easy; it is simply a process of tracking each program and identifying the amount saved.

It is far more difficult to evaluate the impact of the cost-saving move on quality and customer satisfaction; these changes are often subtle and hard to see. Will anyone notice if there is a little less ketchup on a hamburger? Even if they notice, will anyone care? Although the answer to both of these questions may be no, a series of small moves like this can ultimately result in low-quality products and weak brands. Proceed with caution!

10. INTRODUCE A NEW BRAND

Launching a new brand is one of the biggest investments a company can make; the cost of gaining distribution, creating awareness, building trial, and securing repeat is substantial. Creating a new brand is also an incredibly powerful way to drive growth. It is a high-risk and high-reward proposition.

In almost all cases, a new brand should have its own marketing plan, highlighting how it will succeed in the market and laying out priorities for the launch. However, a new brand will almost always be a strategic initiative in a broader marketing plan.

TACTICS

Many things go into successfully launching a new brand; the topic warrants a book all on its own. It is important to remember, however, that four things are essential if a new brand is to succeed. First, the brand needs to gain awareness; people have to know it exists. Second, the brand has to secure distribution; customers have to have access to it. Third, the brand has to gain trial. And fourth, people have to come back and purchase the brand's product again. Each of these tasks needs dedicated tactics.

MEASUREMENT

The success of a new brand is fairly simple to measure by tracking revenue or sales, the numbers that matter most during a launch. Ultimately profit will matter most, of course, but during the launch, sales are a better indicator; without sales, there of course will be no profits.

Revenue doesn't say much about why a new brand is succeeding or why it's not. Revenue is simply the result. It is therefore important to measure other things, such as awareness and distribution and trial. These things do not matter on their own, but they are important diagnostics for understanding how well the new product is doing.

11. ATTRACT COMPETITORS' CUSTOMERS

One sure way to build a business is to steal your competitors' customers. Many markets are, to some degree, zero-sum games; the more you grow, the more your competition loses, and vice versa. As a result, directly targeting your competition can be a powerful approach.

TACTICS

You can attract your competition's customers primarily in two ways: with incentives and with messages. Incentives include all the different offers and promotions you can use to bring in your competition's customers. For example, a bank might offer a large cash payment for new customers who open a direct-deposit checking account; these people are probably just switching from another bank. Similarly, a credit card may offer zero percent interest for new customers. Again, this offer is for people switching from the competition.

Messages include all the things a company can say about a product or service to get someone to switch. This might include highlighting unique features in the product or service, or direct product comparisons. One of the most famous examples of this is the Pepsi Challenge, a head-to-head product comparison of Coke and Pepsi.

Targeting is critical when it comes to going after your competitors' customers; you want to focus your message exclusively on that group. In many cases, you do not want to reach your current customers with the same effort; a high-value trial promotion might be effective at getting your competition's customers to purchase your product, but you don't want to give your current customers the same offer because it would be highly inefficient.

The risk in targeting your competition's customers is that you can quickly get into a competitive battle, with each company offering big incentives for people to switch and attacking other products.

This can lead to lots of inefficient switching and damage the entire category.

MEASUREMENT

It can be difficult to measure this strategic initiative for two reasons. First, it is often hard to identify how many new customers are coming into the franchise. Second, it often isn't clear where a new customer comes from; is it someone new to the category, or someone switching from the competition?

Nonetheless, it is important to measure something. If it isn't possible to identify actual customers coming from the competition, the focus should shift to total customer count (also called penetration) and overall sales.

12. DEFEND AGAINST A NEW COMPETITIVE PRODUCT

A company with a strong position in an attractive market needs to defend its position. In many cases, there will be a steady stream of competitive attacks, as different companies attempt to get a piece of the action. Ensuring that the challengers fail to establish a place in the market is a critically important task. Any time a meaningful new competitor shows up, a company should mount a defensive effort.

TACTICS

The goal in most defensive efforts is clear: Kill the attacker. This isn't pleasant work; it is tough and brutal. Companies don't like to discuss defensive efforts for obvious reasons; there is a fine line between a tough fight and illegal anticompetitive behavior.

When considering defensive programs, it is useful to remember that every business has to make money; this is the goal of essentially every for-profit organization in the world. As a result, the mission of a defender is to convince the attacker that it will be impossible to make money with the new initiative. If a defender can blow up the attacker's financial proposition, the attacker will stop. People don't do things to lose money.

A defensive effort needs to consider timing. Every new product has to do four things: gain distribution, build awareness, build trial, and secure repeat. These are basically sequential, as one step leads to the next. A company can defend at each step. Tactics vary depending on timing; trade incentives may be an effective way to block distribution but will do little to impact repeat. Loading programs are powerful tools for limiting trial but won't have a big impact on awareness.

MEASUREMENT

Defensive efforts can be hard to measure because the objective is to affect someone else's results. Still, it is usually possible to get at least some indication of how the attacker is doing. A defensive goal might be limiting the attacker to a certain share of a category or a certain amount of revenue, or it could even be the demise of the competitive product entirely.

13. ENTER A NEW MARKET

Entering a new market is an obvious way to build a business. If you expand into a new city, region, or country, you will attract new customers and build sales and profits. This is the theory, at least. The reality is often challenging, indeed.

TACTICS

Entering a new market is very much like launching a new product. In the new area, your product really is just another new business.

As a result, the same four new-product steps apply: gain distribution, build awareness, get trial, and secure repeat. Each of these steps requires effort and thought, and different tactics drive each one. Building distribution requires incentives and a sales organization. Gaining awareness depends on advertising and public relations efforts. Trial depends on sampling and incentives. Repeat depends on incentives and reminders.

MEASUREMENT

The success of a launch in a new geography is easy to determine by monitoring sales and market share versus the plan.

As with any new product, it is wise to supplement sales with other measures because sales looks at the total impact; it is not diagnostic. There are other measures that can help diagnose what is working and what is not: it is possible to measure distribution, awareness, trial, and repeat.

14. INCREASE REFERRALS

Referrals can be essential for a business; in some categories, referrals play a critically important role in driving trial. Dentists, for example, depend heavily on referrals for new patients. Consultants, accountants, financial planners, and churches are all businesses for which referrals are a key lever.

Increasing referrals is a logical strategic initiative for many businesses; for a dentist, an increase in referrals will lead directly to an increase in new patients. It could also lead to an increase in loyalty among people doing the referring—people who refer are often the most loyal.

TACTICS

It can be difficult to build referrals. It is possible to build awareness of a brand simply by buying a lot of advertising and getting in front of people. Similarly, it is possible to build trial with very heavy incentives aimed at new customers. Referrals, however, are harder to get because they are largely out of the control of the organization.

It is possible, however, to encourage referrals through different marketing moves. Incentives such as a discount if someone refers a friend can certainly motivate someone, though this incentive may reduce the impact of the referral somewhat. It is better simply to ask customers, "So who else might need this service?" or "Will you recommend me to your colleagues?" Pharmaceutical giant Merck aggressively sought referrals during the 2007 launch of its vaccine Gardasil, running ads asking people to "Tell Someone."

MEASUREMENT

It is difficult to measure how often your brand is being referred to other people, although there are ways to evaluate the success of a referral campaign.

As referrals should lead to new customers, it is possible to track the number of new customers to see if it is increasing after the launch of a referral campaign.

More directly, you can ask new customers how they heard about the brand or the company, and note what share of new customers mention a referral.

15. REPOSITION THE BRAND

Repositioning a brand is a classic strategic initiative. Brands are not always a positive; brands can be negative, neutral, or positive. As a result, sometimes it is necessary to deliberately change what a brand means. A brand that stands for cheap products and low quality may find that this is a difficult set of associations to work with. A brand that seems old may well fail to attract younger people.

If a brand has a negative image, or a negative set of associations that is hurting the business, there are only two viable options. The first option is to change the associations, or reposition the brand. The second option is to give up on the brand entirely. The second option is, for obvious reasons, not appealing.

Not every repositioning will succeed because it can be very difficult to change the associations around a well-known and established brand. Getting people to think of Walmart as a place to buy fashionable products would be difficult. General Motors has been trying to reposition its Cadillac brand for many years with somewhat limited success. And it will be a long time before people see Iraq as a peaceful, prosperous nation.

Still, given the alternatives, repositioning can be a critical strategic initiative for a business with a weak brand.

TACTICS

The challenge in repositioning a brand is that existing customers may leave faster than new customers arrive. Any time the associations around a brand change, some customers will stop using the brand, deciding they liked the old one better than the new one. This is inevitable. The challenge is that if the existing customers leave all at once, the financial results on a brand can deteriorate quickly. But attracting new people to a brand takes time. People won't rush to a brand simply because the packaging and the advertising changed; it takes time to earn credibility. As a result, a brand going through a repositioning may well lose sales at such a pace that the business begins to implode. This is a substantial risk.

Virtually everything that a business does has an impact on the brand, which means almost every tactic can be deployed in a repositioning. All of the four Ps (product, place, price, and promotion) are up for discussion. The greater the repositioning, the more things will need to change.

Advertising is usually a large part of a brand repositioning effort, because advertising is a uniquely broad-reach vehicle. Few things can match the impact of a well-crafted television campaign. Public relations efforts can play a major role, too, as can endorsements, partnerships, pricing, and packaging. Indeed, virtually any marketing tactic can be deployed to support a repositioning.

MEASUREMENT

It can be a challenge to track the success of a brand repositioning effort for the very simple reason that sales are generally a poor measure. Indeed, during a repositioning, sales frequently decline; current customers may depart quickly while new customers are slow to appear. A sales decline may suggest that the repositioning is not working when the reverse is actually true. Worst case, a repositioning that is going well may appear to be a failure, leading the company to declare the repositioning a flop and reverse course.

The best measures to evaluate a brand repositioning are those that look at the image of a brand and the composition of the brand franchise. For example, a change in the associations around a brand could be a major indicator of success for a repositioning. Similarly, a change in the group of people buying a brand might indicate success; for a brand attempting to attract a younger consumer base, a drop in the average age of the franchise would be a step forward.

It is essential to set modest targets for a repositioning because it takes time and effort. Repositionings do not yield fruit quickly.

16. ENTER A NEW DISTRIBUTION CHANNEL

Entering a new distribution channel can be a very effective way to drive incremental sales and reach new customers. Tractor maker John Deere, for example, relied exclusively on its own dealers for many years. In 2005, however, the company started selling through mass retailers such as Home Depot. This move built sales and broadened the customer base because John Deere tractors were now readily available to a much larger group of people.

Changes in a distribution system are major moves because they usually have a long-term impact. In addition, these moves can increase sales substantially. They can also create conflict among channels and bring about complexity. In addition, a distribution channel decision can have a major impact on the brand, for better or for worse. The challenge is to evaluate the potential for incremental gain versus the increased risk of conflict and confusion and damage to the brand.

TACTICS

Entering a new channel is a major undertaking; it requires focus and determination. In most cases, tactics supporting the expansion include an expanded sales effort and promotional incentives. The expansion, however, may also require a broader marketing effort to inform consumers of the change, including advertising and online marketing.

During the expansion to new channels, it is important to focus on existing channels, too; declines in the existing channel can easily overwhelm any gains from the new channel.

MEASUREMENT

Progress in the new channel is easy to measure, because sales volume is a basic indicator of success. By setting a clear sales target, it is easy to see how things are going with the new initiative. More defined measures, such as level of distribution and sales velocity, can also help monitor success and diagnose what precisely is happening.

It is more difficult to measure how the distribution change is affecting the entire franchise. Cannibalization can be hard to see. For example, are declines in the existing channel due to people moving to the new channel? Or is the existing channel not executing well? Or is the category simply declining overall?

As a result, it is important to establish measures for the existing channel. In particular, it is essential to gather customer-level information through customer surveys so that you can evaluate how growth in one channel is affecting the other.

17. INCREASE PRICING

Increasing prices is perhaps the world's most perfect marketing move. It is simple, quick, certain, and quantifiable. It requires no capital investment, no R&D work, and no creative development.

More importantly, it can have a dramatic impact on a business. If a business has a bottom-line margin of 5 percent, then a tiny 1 percent increase in price will increase profits by 20 percent, less the impact of sales declines.

There are problems with price increases, of course. In almost all cases, a price increase will result in lower sales, and for some businesses, the gains from a price increase can be overwhelmed by the resulting losses in volume, so the price increase ends up increasing profits only slightly, or actually decreases profits. The key question is price elasticity. A business with very high price elasticity will find it difficult to justify a price increase because sales volumes will fall off substantially as prices go up. A business with low price elasticity will profit handsomely from an increase in price because sales will fall only slightly with a price increase.

This is why it is so important to have differentiation on a business. Businesses that are highly differentiated and preferred by customers generally have lower price elasticity. Businesses that lack differentiation have high price elasticity.

TACTICS

Increasing prices is usually a very simple matter: just do it. This is one of the reasons pricing is such a wonderful tactic. It's about as basic as it gets.

But it is important to keep in mind several factors when raising prices. First, timing can be important. When should you announce a price increase? When is it effective? Generally, customers will stock up if they know a price increase is coming. This will lead to a sharp increase in sales, followed by a decline as customers work down their inventory. This volume swing can create operational issues and financial issues, so it is important to manage the size of the buyout by reducing the time customers have to buy at the old price and capping the amount customers can purchase at the old price.

Second, channel issues may make pricing difficult. Many companies sell to distributors or retailers, not to the end customer. In this case, it is important to think through how the price increase will be received. Will distributors push back? Will they use the price increase as a chance to increase their prices, too? Understanding how distribution partners will react to the price increase is essential to ensure success.

Third, it is critical to think about how competitors will react to the price increase. You can't talk to your competitors about pricing; this is generally illegal and unethical. However, it is important to think about how they will react to the price increase. Will they follow your increase or not? What usually happens in the market? Being aware of the category norms and pricing history is important to ensure that your pricing move is optimal from a competitive perspective.

MEASUREMENT

For most businesses, pricing is easy to see. Indeed, it isn't even necessary to evaluate whether or not the price increase is in place: if prices are up, then prices are up.

In some cases pricing is not quite so obvious. If a sales force has the ability to negotiate prices, then ensuring that prices actually go up requires evaluation, and monitoring this becomes important.

There are several things to watch and measure, however, as the price increase flows into the market. First, it is critical to watch competition. Did your competitors match the pricing move? Any price move should have assumptions about likely competitive response. Once the price increase is in place, it is possible to see if competition is acting as expected.

Second, if you sell through distributors or retailers, it is important to consider their response. Did they pass on the price increase? Are prices to end customers going up? Is the increase more than you expected or less?

Third, it is critical to watch how pricing is affecting sales. Seeing this, however, can be difficult; sales on a business are driven by many things, so identifying precisely the impact of the price increase can be hard. It is generally possible, however, to see major shifts, such as a major and abrupt drop in sales.

18. STRENGTHEN THE BRAND

Building a brand is a key marketing task; for many companies, brands are the most important assets. A common and important marketing initiative is strengthening the brand, ensuring that customers prefer it to others. Brand loyalty is both powerful and enduring.

TACTICS

Every point of contact a person has with a brand shapes his associations with it. So while advertising certainly has a major impact on a brand, a marketer must also consider customer service, public relations, and every other place customers see or interact with the brand.

There are many tactics that can build a brand, and they should be based on an understanding of the customer and the brand. Once you know how customers feel about your brand, it is possible to develop tactics that can strengthen the relationship.

For example, if customers know and like your brand but don't see it as different from the competition, it would be natural to highlight points of difference through communication vehicles. If customers understand your brand but don't feel particularly connected to it, you could create ways for people to become more involved in the brand through events and other engaging activities.

MEASUREMENT

Measuring the strength of a brand can be a challenge. A brand is a set of associations linked to a name, mark, or symbol. The challenge in measurement is to evaluate the strength and nature of these associations and, in particular, see how they change as your marketing effort unfolds.

The best way to measure a brand is through quantitative techniques, such as consumer surveys, that ask about brand awareness, brand perceptions, and brand purchase intent.

It can be very hard to see the impact of a marketing campaign aimed at strengthening associations because well-established brands change very slowly. As a result, the changes can sometimes be impossible to see in a quantitative survey; the margin of error in the survey may obscure the impact of the campaign. This doesn't necessarily mean the campaign is not working. Setting modest goals is important in a campaign to strengthen the brand. Indeed, it is best to monitor the tactics, such as attendance at events or visits to a website, in addition to the core brand equity measures.

19. TEST NEW MARKETING TACTICS

The best way to learn about new marketing tactics is to try them. Simply talking about potential ideas is insufficient. Until you actually try something, you won't know for sure if the tactic will work for your business or not. As a result, testing is critical; you have to try new things.

Any business leader responsible for delivering financial results faces a very simple problem. Old marketing tactics may not work particularly well, but they are generally predictable and certain. If you rely on the proven levers, chances are good that you will reach your goals. It might not be optimal, but you will probably get there. New marketing tactics might be much better than the old tactics, but the new tactics are uncertain and unproven. They might be better, but then again they might be worse. If you bet on the new tactics, you might be a hero, but you also might be a dog; there is a very good chance you will miss your plan—an unappealing proposition.

The tension between the old, predictable tactics and the new, unproven tactics explains why many new marketing techniques catch on so slowly. Why take the risk?

For prudent marketers, the only way to embrace new things is to try them in a modest way while maintaining the proven tactics. If the new tactics prove to be effective, then a more dramatic shift in spending will be both safe and effective.

TACTICS

Every day, it seems, there are more ways to promote and market a product. You now can put stickers on bananas, videos on the Internet, and holographs in a train station. The options go on and on. Most of them are interesting and cool and appealing.

The challenge is that it is impossible to test all of the new tactics; there are simply too many. In addition, each test takes time and money, both of which are limited.

The first step in experimenting with new tactics is to identify the most attractive options; it is possible to sift through the options and identify which tactics are even remotely feasible for your brand.

Usually there are three things to consider. First, is the tactic scalable? In other words, will the tactic ever be big enough to matter? Some tactics are so small that in the end they will never have enough of an impact to really matter. Second, does it fit with your brand? Some tactics are simply inconsistent with a brand. An ad posted above a urinal is not the best place for Tiffany or McKinsey to be advertising. Third, do the economics make any sense? If there is no possible way a marketing tactic would be a smart financial decision, there is no reason to try it.

Once the tactics have been narrowed down, it is possible to identify the options with the greatest potential and move those into testing.

MEASUREMENT

The most important thing to remember when evaluating new marketing tactics is that the metrics must be clear before you field the test. It is very hard to figure out after the fact if a marketing program was a success or not if you didn't establish the measures ahead of time. What is success, anyway?

For any marketing test, then, creating clear metrics is essential. The best measure, of course, is sales. How did the new tactic impact revenue and profit? Getting this information is easier said than done, however, so you will often need to have a secondary measure, such as phone calls or hits to a website. But you have something you can measure to determine if the tactic is successful or not.

20. ACCELERATE NEW-PRODUCT DEVELOPMENT

Creating a new product takes time and energy and focus. As a result, if new-product development is important for a business, it may well show up as a strategic initiative in the marketing plan. This initiative is more about creating products than actually putting them into the market; accelerating new-product development will, with luck, lead to new product launches in later years. If new products are an important part of the long-term plan, however, ramping up new-product development today is an important strategic initiative. If you don't get to work, the new products will never appear.

TACTICS

While new-product development requires a mix of art and science, it is very possible to take concrete steps to accelerate the process. These steps range from establishing a cross-functional team, to hiring people with the necessary product development skills, to providing resources and fielding concept and product tests.

Putting a formal new-product development process into place is an important action step. The most common new-product development process involves stages and gates. Before an idea can move from one stage to the next, it has to make it through a particular gate. So before an idea can move from the concept development stage to the feasibility stage, for example, it has to have positive concept test results. And before a product can move from the feasibility stage into the product development stage, the basic financial proposition has to work.

MEASUREMENT

Evaluating the success of a new-product development process is fairly easy if there is a formal process in place; it is possible to track the number of ideas at the different stages of the development process. For example, an organization could set a goal of having three different ideas make it to the product development stage by a certain time. It then becomes very easy to assess whether the new-products process is on track or behind.

Moreover, simply putting a product development process into place could be a key milestone.

* * *

No strategic initiative is right for every business. Each business has unique challenges at a given time, and what works for one may not work for another. That is what makes building a business so challenging. The key is to be aware of the wide range of available options and use the marketing planning process to identify the initiatives that have the best chance of driving your business forward.

Chapter 10

MARKETING PLAN TEMPLATE

THERE IS NO ONE SINGLE FORMAT for a marketing plan. Some marketing plans are written documents and some are presentations. Some plans are lengthy and detailed, while others are short and concise. Some marketing plans are never formally written down; they are scribbled on a napkin in a restaurant.

This makes a lot of sense because a plan needs to fit the situation. An organization that makes decisions in meetings should create a marketing plan in a presentation format. A company that uses memos should write out the marketing plan. A complicated business will probably have a more detailed plan than a simple business; a marketing plan for Microsoft Office will obviously need to be longer and more detailed than one for a small neighborhood restaurant.

At the core, though, most good marketing plans follow the same basic flow. This is true whether they are written or presented, long or short, formal or informal.

What follows are two tools to help craft a breakthrough marketing plan. The first is a general outline, showing what should be in a plan and how the material should generally flow. The second is a detailed, page-by-page template for a presented plan. The template shows precisely what the pages in a marketing plan presentation should look like.

One note of caution: Both the outline and the template should be used as starting points. Indeed, providing a template for a marketing plan is a little dangerous; the risk is that people will simply fill in the pages instead of thinking about the situation facing the business or giving adequate time to crafting the story that explains where the business is at the moment and justifies the plan of attack. The goal, ultimately, is not to follow one template or another; it is to create a marketing plan that sets a smart strategic course for the business in a compelling way so that people support it.

MARKETING PLAN OUTLINE

The outline below presents the key parts of a marketing plan. This can be used whether the plan is a presentation or a written document. Think of this as a starting point for creating a plan.

1. TITLE PAGE

A marketing plan should always start with a title page. This probably seems obvious, but it is all too often overlooked.

A title page should include the name of the business, the date the plan was submitted or presented, the people on the team who worked on it, and of course the title, which is usually something catchy like this: British Airways 2014 Marketing Plan.

Each element is important. The name of the business is essential; you have to know what is being discussed. The date is also important because, in most cases, there will be several versions of the marketing plan floating around, each one updated and revised slightly. It can be difficult to identify the latest version if the date isn't on the plan.

Putting the names of the team members on the title page does three good things. First, it clarifies who precisely created the plan. This is usually quite obvious at the time a plan is presented. However, marketing plans tend to hang around for years and years. Five years after the presentation, it is often hard to figure out who was on the team at the time. With the names on the title page, it is clear who worked on it, and it then becomes easy to follow up with those people if need be.

Second, including names on the title page cements commitment from the team; it is hard to disagree with a plan when your name is on the cover. This can be very powerful. People often take deep interest in a document when their name is on it. There is no better way to ensure support.

Third, including names makes it easy to share the credit. It is a reward, in a sense, for the people who spent time thinking about and creating the plan. People generally like to be recognized. Without their name on the plan, people may feel the need to actually present something in the final meeting to show everyone that they, too, contributed to the plan and were part of the process. This can lead to choppy and disjointed presentations.

2. EXECUTIVE SUMMARY

It is always best to lead with an executive summary that highlights the key points in the plan; this should follow immediately after the title page.

When I was a child, I was a member of my local 4-H club. I raised pigs and sheep, caught butterflies, and built birdhouses. And each year I gave a presentation in the public speaking program. One year I gave a talk about washing chickens, another year I discussed raising ducks, and another year I explored the topic of collecting beetles.

One of the things I learned from those presentations was the power of a good summary. If I started with a short summary of my key points, the presentation almost always went well and I received a blue ribbon at the end of the day. The classic line is really true: tell people what you are going to tell them, tell them, and then tell them what you just told them.

I also learned that bringing a chicken to a presentation is a good way to get people's attention and win them over. That lesson is a bit harder to apply in the corporate world, but if you think creatively, you probably can identify something that will have a similar effect.

If you begin your marketing plan with a summary, you are off to a very good start. The summary should be short and focused, highlighting the key parts of the plan, including the goals and strategic initiatives. In a presentation, the executive summary should ideally be just one page, and it should never be longer than two pages.

The summary does several things. Most important, it gets the point across. Many people can't focus for long periods; there is simply too much going on and too many smart phones. If you put the main points of your plan at the end of the document, there is a good chance your audience won't be paying attention. You also might never get to the key point; if your audience has a lot of questions, you could run out of time and have to rush through the most important points, or fail to deliver them at all.

An executive summary also helps the people in your audience because it gives them a preview of what is coming up. This helps them figure out how to listen to the presentation. If the plan seems reasonable, for example, an executive might decide to say very little, provide some encouragement, and stay away from the details; there is no need to debate the fine points of an analysis if the overall conclusion makes sense. Why waste the time and energy? If the plan is more questionable, however, an executive will quickly see the need to pay attention and concentrate on the plan's logic and analysis.

The executive summary also sets the tone for the presentation. If the business is in basically good shape and the plan simply builds on this success, then the summary should set a tone of confidence, stability, and optimism. If the business is doing poorly and the marketing plan is a dramatic change from the past, then the tone should be serious and urgent.

The only time a marketing plan should not start with a summary of the plan is when the recommendation is so controversial that putting it up front might cause a strongly negative reaction from the audience, such that people aren't even willing to seriously listen to the plan. In this case, it is best to put the recommendation at the end and build to it. The document would still have an executive summary at the start, but the meat of the recommendation, the controversial part, would be farther back in the document. The introduction should simply set up the need for bold and innovative thinking, but not get into the specifics; those come later.

3. AGENDA

An agenda or table of contents is important even in a small plan, simply to let people know what is coming up and how the presentation will flow.

It is important to let people see what's ahead. For example, senior executives will almost always want to see the financial implications, so it's good to tell them when the topic will be addressed. If you don't do this, they will probably go searching for the financial information or get nervous that you aren't planning to discuss it at all. Without a clear agenda, people may feel the need to jump in and ask about things that will be coming later in the presentation, forcing a presenter to constantly reply, "We'll be getting to that later." This isn't a satisfying response.

In a presentation, the agenda can also serve as an organizing device, nicely dividing sections of the presentation and setting up the story.

The table of contents is best positioned right after the executive summary, not before. This is because the summary is usually quite exciting; it highlights the big, interesting news. It is always best to start a recommendation on a positive note. The agenda isn't thrilling; people can focus on it once they know the basics of the plan.

4. STATE OF THE BUSINESS

Before you can build a house, you need to lay the foundation. This is what the house is built on; without a solid foundation, you can't create a strong, stable structure. This is also true with marketing plans; you need to lay the foundation before you can construct the plan.

A good foundation in a marketing plan ensures that there is a common understanding of the business. There should be three things in this section of the plan: the vision and positioning, an update on recent results, and the business challenge.

The vision and positioning should be the stable core of a business. The vision speaks to the values of the organization and its long-term direction. The positioning clarifies precisely how the brand competes in the market. It is important to be clear on both before getting into the details of the plan.

In a marketing plan presentation, the vision and brand positioning should not be anything new. The point is simply to review what is in place. If you don't have a positioning for a particular brand, you should figure it out before creating and presenting your marketing plan. Presenting a new positioning statement in a marketing plan is not a smart approach; it will likely derail the discussion entirely because positioning is difficult, and positioning debates can go on and on and on.

A marketing plan must include an update on how the business is doing; it has to be written with an understanding of results. A business that is doing well faces certain issues, and a business that is not doing well faces very different issues. Being clear on this is important; everyone reviewing the plan has to agree on how the business is performing before reviewing the plan, just as physicians have to agree on a diagnosis before debating the correct treatment course.

The recent results section should be a brief recap of how the business is performing. This is not the time to present new information. If you start a marketing plan presentation by announcing that the business is doing much better than expected, you will simply derail the discussion; people will likely focus on understanding why things are going so well, not on the plan for the future.

Finally, the foundation should identify the key challenge or two facing the business. Big picture, what is the main issue the plan has to address? The challenge might be accelerating growth, or maintaining momentum, or building margins in a declining category, or battling a competitive entrant. Clarity on this is critical.

Every business faces challenges. Businesses that are doing poorly, of course, face the challenge of turning around the business. Very simply, how will management get the business on the right track? Businesses that are doing well also face challenges, and in some ways these are more difficult. How will the business continue to grow? What will sustain the momentum over time?

The challenge section is important because it lays the groundwork for the rest of the plan. Every point in this section should be considered because the recommended plan builds off this material. Issues you identify early in the plan document need to be addressed later. If you note that the rising cost of commodities is a big concern, for example, then the plan needs to respond to this somehow.

The business challenge section of the plan should be short and focused. In a presentation, the vision and positioning should generally take a page, the results review should take one or two pages, and the challenge should take one or two pages. The goal is to highlight how the business is performing and the challenges ahead, not to present mounds of data about the business.

5. GOALS/OBJECTIVES

The goals/objectives section should present the one or two key targets for the upcoming period. One objective should almost always be centered on profit, and sometimes that is sufficient. In most cases, however, a business will have another goal or two in addition to profit, such as increasing market share, improving brand perception, or establishing a presence in a new market.

The objectives should not be a surprise for the audience; you should communicate these in advance so that this section is just a review, confirming that the objectives are correct. This is sort of a routine check, much as flight attendants do a destination check before closing the plane doors.

Indeed, if there is disagreement on the objectives, there is no point in proceeding with the rest of the plan; a marketing plan created to achieve one set of objectives will rarely be appropriate to achieve a different set of objectives.

The objectives section should be short; in a presentation it should be at most one or two pages.

6. STRATEGIC INITIATIVES

The strategic initiatives section is the heart of the plan. This is where you present the top priorities for the business.

In many ways, the strategic initiatives are the most important part of a marketing plan, so this section needs to be robust. You should present each initiative clearly and support it with a strong rationale. Why is this initiative important? What is the data that supports this?

There are times when an initiative will require extensive supporting analysis; this is fine. If you recommend that building share in the northeastern part of the United States should be the top priority, then you'll need to show why the Northeast matters so much. This will require an analysis of the different geographic regions. Similarly, if you recommend entering a new segment of the market, then you'll have to justify why this segment is so appealing, and more appealing than other opportunities.

7. TACTICS

Tactics are specific actions. Tactics should always follow initiatives; you shouldn't discuss tactics for building buying rate, for example, until you've established that building buying rate is a priority.

Tactical information should always be summarized; there is rarely enough time to go through all the tactical details. This is true for even the simplest of businesses. A discussion of tactics can go on and on; understanding something as simple as a modest packaging change can take a very long time. In the plan presentation, you should focus on the big moves. What must happen to make each strategic initiative successful? What are the most important tactical moves?

The marketing plan is not the place to discuss details related to execution. In your plan, you might have a tactic "Buy keywords on Google." You shouldn't then get into all the details of this move. You can address questions such as "What words?" and "At what price?"

and "What is the ROI of that?" in a different meeting focused just on that particular tactical move.

8. FINANCIAL IMPLICATIONS

Every marketing plan needs a section on the numbers; failing to connect the marketing plan to the numbers is a major problem. Innovation and strategy are terrific, but ultimately the numbers have to work.

Financials are a priority for every organization, whether for profit or not for profit. A flashy plan that makes enormous sense but has no chance of delivering the financial targets is of little use.

The financial section of a marketing plan should show the overall financial picture. What will happen to spending with this plan? What will happen to revenue and profit? The financial section should address a simple question: If we execute this plan, what is the likely financial outcome?

The financial section should link back to the objectives. In most cases, one of the main goals will be profit. In the financial section, then, the projected results should be compared with the goals. Will this plan deliver the objective? Will it fall short?

The challenge in the financial section is to provide enough information to indicate how the plan will impact the financial outlook without becoming bogged down in the details; a marketing plan is not a detailed budget. In general, a summary income statement is sufficient, showing the most important parts.

9. RISKS AND CONTINGENCIES

Things rarely happen exactly according to plan. Economic forces are hard to predict with great accuracy. Competitors can make unexpected moves. Programs might not work as anticipated.

For this reason, it is important to highlight key risks. What might go wrong? What are the big bets? And what would be the impact?

The goal is not to highlight every possible risk, just the most significant ones. For example, if a new product launch is a critical part of the plan, then a risk might be slower-than-expected uptake on the new item. What happens if the business only gains five share points in the first six months instead of the projected ten points?

It is important to consider contingency moves when dealing with risks. If risk A actually occurs, how will you respond? What will be the impact of the response? Ideally, you are able to identify contingency moves that offset the financial impact. So if the new product fails to gain share, you reduce spending on another initiative in order to offset the financial miss.

One can also highlight opportunities, things that might go better than expected and provide upside. This can be a useful exercise, too. In my experience, however, risks materialize far more frequently than opportunities.

10. MILESTONES

This section presents key milestones for the business. It answers a rather basic question: How do we know if we are on track? To get great execution, a business needs benchmarks to monitor progress and indicate if things are coming together.

A business can't have fifty milestones. The focus of this section is to highlight a few key things to watch as the year unfolds.

If a marketing plan calls for a big new product introduction, for example, then key milestones might include getting positive test results, developing good advertising, and gaining a certain amount of distribution. If reducing costs is important, then the milestones might highlight that by the end of the first quarter, the specific cost saving ideas have to be clear.

11. EXECUTIVE SUMMARY

A marketing plan should finish with a reprise of the executive summary, recapping the key points.

People often neglect the end of the plan, figuring that by the time the end appears everyone will be so tired that it is best to simply walk off and get back to work. This is absolutely not the case; the summary, or the end of a marketing plan, is critical. After all the plan's details, the challenge is to bring the audience back to the main points so that everyone leaves with the core messages top of mind.

One approach that works well is to simply repeat the executive summary from the beginning of the plan, so the same material begins and ends the document. This is very effective because it provides strong bookends. It also makes the summary the most important part in the plan, which of course it is.

MARKETING PLAN TEMPLATE

The marketing plan template that follows can serve as a basic guide to laying out a marketing plan. Remember, though, that it is just a starting point; managers should modify it as needed. Completing a template is helpful, but it will only work if the plan tells a compelling story.

Exhibit 10.1   Marketing Plan Template

2014 Marketing Plan Product

Date
Presenters
Location

Agenda

1. Executive Summary
2. State of the Business
3. Goals/Objectives
4. Strategic Initiatives
5. Tactics
6. Financial Implications
7. Risks and Contingencies
8. Milestones
9. Summary

Agenda

1. Executive Summary
2. State of the Business
3. Goals/Objectives
4. Strategic Initiatives
5. Tactics
6. Financial Implications
7. Risks and Contingencies
8. Milestones
9. Summary

Executive Summary

This page should summarize the overall plan in several bullets.

The executive summary should generally be just one page. It should never be more than two pages.

Agenda

1. Executive Summary
2. State of the Business
3. Goals/Objectives
4. Strategic Initiatives
5. Tactics
6. Financial Implications
7. Risks and Contingencies
8. Milestones
9. Summary

Vision and Brand Positioning

This page should present the vision and positioning. This should not be new information; it should simply be a reminder.

Recent Results

This page should provide an update on the business to set the stage for the plan to follow.

Key things to address:- How is the business performing?
- What are the key drivers of recent results?

In general, this should not be new information. It should just be a recap of the situation.

This section might require several pages.

Business Challenge

This page should summarize the core challenge facing the business going forward.

The challenge will usually be linked to recent results. For example, if results have been weak due to competitive spending, the core challenge may well be how to deal with the competitive situation.

Agenda

1. Executive Summary
2. State of the Business
3. Goals/Objectives
4. Strategic Initiatives
5. Tactics
6. Financial Implications
7. Risks and Contingencies
8. Milestones
9. Summary

Goals/Objectives

This page should present the objectives for the business, such as revenue growth or profit growth.

The objectives should not be a surprise to the audience.

It is best to have only one or two objectives.

Agenda

1. Executive Summary
2. State of the Business
3. Goals/Objectives
4. Strategic Initiatives
5. Tactics
6. Financial Implications
7. Risks and Contingencies
8. Milestones
9. Summary

Strategic Initiatives

This section presents the strategic initiatives that will drive the business. What needs to happen to achieve the objective?

Strategic initiatives are always actions, such as driving trial on a new product or building loyalty among heavy users.

The section should explain why each initiative is important.

It is best to have three or four strategic initiatives.

This section could include several pages, perhaps one page per initiative.

Agenda

1. Executive Summary
2. State of the Business
3. Goals/Objectives
4. Strategic Initiatives
5. Tactics
6. Financial Implications
7. Risks and Contingencies
8. Milestones
9. Summary

Tactics

This section presents the tactics supporting each strategic initiative. For example, a strategic initiative of building awareness might have tactics such as advertising and local events.

Each initiative should have tactics and each tactic should be linked to an initiative.

Tactical recommendations should be supported by rationale. Why are you recommending a particular tactic?

This section can be split into several pages. For example, each initiative could have a separate page.

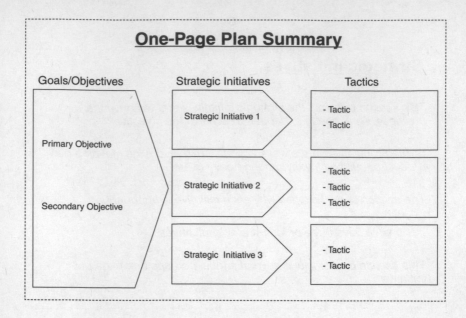

One-Page Plan Summary

Goals/Objectives	Strategic Initiatives	Tactics
Primary Objective	Strategic Initiative 1	- Tactic - Tactic
Secondary Objective	Strategic Initiative 2	- Tactic - Tactic - Tactic
	Strategic Initiative 3	- Tactic - Tactic

Agenda

1. Executive Summary
2. State of the Business
3. Goals/Objectives
4. Strategic Initiatives
5. Tactics
6. Financial Implications
7. Risks and Contingencies
8. Milestones
9. Summary

Financial Implications

This section should show the financial outlook.

What will happen to spending? What will happen to revenue? Profit?

This should not be a detailed, elaborate set of financial projections; doing a detailed budget is a distinct step in the process.

Agenda

1. Executive Summary
2. State of the Business
3. Goals/Objectives
4. Strategic Initiatives
5. Tactics
6. Financial Implications
7. Risks and Contingencies
8. Milestones
9. Summary

Risks and Contingencies

Risks   Contingencies

This section should show the risks.

What might to wrong? If this happens, what is the backup plan?

Agenda

1. Executive Summary
2. State of the Business
3. Goals/Objectives
4. Strategic Initiatives
5. Tactics
6. Financial Implications
7. Risks and Contingencies
8. Milestones
9. Summary

Milestones

Milestone   Date

What needs to happen for the plan to work? What are the key dates?

There should only be a few key milestones.

Summary

This page should recap the key points.

It is similar to the executive summary at the beginning. The simplest approach is to repeat the same page.

Chapter 11

COMMON QUESTIONS

OVER THE PAST SEVERAL YEARS, I've taught more than a thousand people how to create powerful marketing plans. During that time, a few questions came up again and again. I answer many of them below.

HOW LONG SHOULD A MARKETING PLAN BE?

This question has two easy and somewhat unsatisfying answers. The first is the old favorite: It depends. The second is equally unsatisfying but more truthful: A marketing plan should be just as long as it needs to be to communicate the goals or objectives, strategic initiatives, and key tactics and to provide compelling support. If you can do this in twenty pages, fine. If it takes you thirty pages, fine. If you can pull it off in four really good pages, even better.

The most important thing to remember is that a marketing plan should not go on and on. If you find yourself creating a one-hundred-page document, immediately stop, step back, and think about what really matters. In many cases, you'll find that the plan is full of information that simply isn't relevant or important. If that is the case, cut the unnecessary material and get to the point. At the very least, move it to the appendix.

In almost all cases, a shorter marketing plan is going to be better than a longer one. Short plans force you to focus. It is difficult to get too confused in a ten-page plan; there simply isn't room. Shorter plans are also easy to produce, so you and your team can focus on analysis and thinking instead of formatting and document creation. Simply typing, printing, and copying a 150-page marketing plan takes a lot of time. The production process can overwhelm the content: "We don't have time to think, we have to start printing!" The lament of one marketing executive with whom I spoke is typical: "I think we do too little work thinking about what will drive the business, and spend too much time writing decks."

Most important, shorter plans are easy to understand. Since the goal of a marketing plan is to communicate a recommendation and gain support, a simple plan is more likely to be understood and to work. As Adobe's Mark Delman observed, "It has to be short. Length allows people to be sloppy. Brevity forces clarity."

Speaking coach Steve Adubato highlighted the problem with long presentations. When asked about a 111-slide presentation, he remarked, "That's not content. That is laziness. What that is saying is, 'If I dump a ton of information on you, I am going to make it look like I did my homework.' Well, you want to know what? Your board is not going to be impressed. I think we confuse volume—quantity of information—with making a real connection."[1]

After a certain point, each additional page detracts from the whole; it diminishes the focus, waters down the story, and increases the chances that your audience will get distracted. Private equity investor Andy Whitman notes that length is sometimes a sign of weak thinking. He explains, "If it takes you eighty pages to cover something, I wonder if there are any ideas in there."

CAN I JUST PRESENT THE PLAN SUMMARY PAGE?

One way to keep things short is to just present one page, the marketing plan summary, showing goals, initiatives, and tactics. This is tempting; it certainly is efficient and gets to the point.

Unfortunately, this is rarely enough. Remember that a good marketing plan has to be convincing. You have to lay out the plan and then provide compelling support for the recommendations. If you have just one page to work with, it is impossible to include supporting points. You might be able to highlight what you are recommending, but you certainly won't be able to explain why the plan will work.

HOW OFTEN SHOULD A BUSINESS WRITE A MARKETING PLAN?

Most companies create a marketing plan once a year as part of an annual process of setting direction for the business. This is a reasonable approach. Over the course of the year a lot can happen, so taking a fresh look at the marketing plan every year only makes sense.

A better guideline is this: A business should write a marketing plan as often as needed to stay on track. In many cases, this means an annual plan will be sufficient. In some cases, however, the business will need to update the plan far more frequently. Anytime the situation changes substantially, a new marketing plan is in order. If a business is doing much better than expected, for example, it will need a new marketing plan that looks at how to maintain the momentum and evaluates the implications on the full-year financial picture. If a business is struggling, it will certainly need a new marketing plan aimed at delivering better results. Similarly, if there is a major shift in a market, such as a major increase in the price of a key ingredient, then the team should develop a new plan. In an extreme case, a business might need to create a new marketing plan every month.

The need for frequent updates is one reason why short plans are best. It is virtually impossible to quickly update a two-hundred-page plan, but it is easy to modify a plan with eight or fifteen pages.

Although it is important to adjust and respond to changing conditions, a business should avoid making major strategic shifts too frequently. Almost every strategic shift is costly; it requires resources, time, and energy. A series of major moves can create confusion, with demoralized employees and uncoordinated execution.

The foundation of a business should change very infrequently, if at all. Brand positioning, for example, should remain consistent year after year; the positioning provides continuity for the brand over time. A brand that stands for luxury shouldn't embrace a value positioning simply because short-term business results are weak. A brand that stands for top quality for one day, value the next day, and trendy style the next day will quickly come to stand for nothing at all.

HOW SHOULD A GLOBAL BRAND APPROACH MARKETING PLANS?

Global brands pose a challenge. The problem is simple: every geographic market has unique challenges and opportunities. What works in one country may not work in the next, and a program that has a terrific impact on sales in one place might actually cause sales to decline in another.

As a result, a brand needs a different plan in each market. A good marketing plan takes into account the unique dynamics facing a business. As these dynamics change, the marketing plan needs to change. A plan created for the German market isn't going to work well in Mexico or Brazil.

The problem is that brands should be consistent from market to market. A brand shouldn't mean one thing in Colombia and something different in Brazil; this is difficult to manage and is confusing for customers.

The way to ensure that a brand feels the same all around the world is to be certain that all the marketing plans are built on the same foundation. The brand positioning, for example, should be basically the same in every country. A consistent foundation ensures that each marketing plan will support the global brand. The strategic initiatives will probably be different, and the tactics will almost always be different, but the feel of the brand will be the same.

This is how global brands like McDonald's and BMW succeed in different markets. The marketing plans vary, but they are built on a common understanding of what the brand stands for; this connects the various programs.

SHOULD A MARKETING PLAN BE WRITTEN FOR A PRODUCT OR A COMPANY?

Both! A company should have a marketing plan, and a product should have a marketing plan. The plans should be related, of course, but they are written at very different levels.

One extreme is the marketing plan written for a company. This plan outlines how the total organization will compete and grow. It is generally created by the CEO and the senior management team. At Procter & Gamble, for example, CEO A. G. Lafley created a marketing plan for the entire corporation, highlighting the corporate objectives and the corporation's key strategic initiatives. CEO Jeff Immelt did the same thing at General Electric.

The other extreme is a product marketing plan. This plan lays out how a particular product will compete and achieve its objectives. The objectives are developed at a product level, with strategic initiatives appropriate for the product.

Bigger businesses, of course, have broader strategic initiatives. At the corporate level, a strategic initiative might be something like, "Grow volume in emerging markets." At a product level, a strategic initiative could be, "Win the key holiday week in-store." At both levels, however, the strategic initiatives clearly convey action and direction.

Exhibit 11.1 Marketing Plan Pyramid

Marketing plans within a larger company form a pyramid. Product-level plans are the narrowest. Category marketing plans bring together several product plans. Division plans span several categories. The total company marketing plan builds off the division-level plans. At each level, the plans focus on the most important initiatives. Improving product quality on a particular product might be a strategic initiative for a particular product, but not a big enough strategic initiative to be one of the key priorities for the division or the company (see Exhibit 11.1).

WHAT DO I DO IF MY BOSS IS GIVING ME AN UNREALISTIC PROFIT GOAL?

An achievable profit target is essential. Missing the goal is discouraging. You won't get your bonus, and you'll spend the year scrambling to boost the numbers.

If you think your target isn't achievable, you should push for a more realistic one. You should go through key assumptions with the senior executives to understand why there is a difference of opinion. You should clearly state your case.

Jim Kilts, former CEO of Nabisco, Kraft, and Gillette, recommends leaving if you can't get to a reasonable target. He explains, "Regardless of the pressure, resist the temptation to overpromise. Spend the time necessary to understand exactly what your unit can deliver over time and on a sustained basis. If your bosses don't agree, you have a problem, and your future might be better elsewhere."[2] This is a fairly extreme position, but it highlights the importance of getting the target right.

DOESN'T A PLAN NEED A SITUATION ANALYSIS?

It is essential to understand the situation facing a brand; you can't make good decisions without knowing the dynamics of a business. But there shouldn't be a situation analysis section in a marketing plan. Indeed, the situation analysis section is one reason so many marketing plans are ineffective.

The theory behind the situation analysis is sound. Understanding what is going on in a market is important because you can't make smart decisions unless you first understand the basic dynamics. Great marketing should be grounded in a deep understanding of the business, the brand, the competition, and the customer. So, theoretically, a situation analysis is a very good thing.

The problem is that people very often confuse the situation analysis section with the actual meat of the marketing plan. Instead of discussing the recommendations, the marketing plan turns into a vast research report, where every aspect of the business is examined at great length in the situation analysis.

I recently read a marketing plan with a situation analysis that included this line: "The corporate headquarters are located at 851 Martin Avenue, Santa Clara, California, 95050, where we house our manufacturing, customer support, software engineering and administrative personnel."[3] Why in the world would this be in a marketing plan? Who reading the plan wouldn't know where the offices are located?

The marketing plan should focus relentlessly on what needs to happen to drive the business forward and why it will work. As a result, I believe that including a situation analysis section in a marketing plan is simply asking for trouble. There is a very good chance the section will grow until it overwhelms the plan.

The reason to write a marketing plan in the first place is to lay out a recommendation, gain support, and communicate with the broader organization. The typical situation analysis doesn't help with any of these things; it is just a collection of facts, figures, and analysis.

It is possible to write a tight, simple, and focused situation analysis that leads logically to the final recommendations. Done well, this approach can be effective. The problem is that it is difficult to do; many people get so lost when writing the situation analysis that the story of the business never emerges.

This doesn't mean that a business leader shouldn't analyze a business. On the contrary, to develop a great marketing plan, the manager needs to understand the business exceptionally well. Someone responsible for formulating a marketing plan should look at the available information and analyze it. All this analysis, however, doesn't go in the plan.

All a marketing plan really needs is a simple setup, a short recap of how the business is doing, and a summary of the challenges ahead.

WHAT IF MY BOSS WANTS TO SEE A LONG, TRADITIONAL PLAN?

Never forget that marketing plans are written for a purpose. One very important reason to create a plan is to get support. As a result, you need to keep your audience in mind; you want your plan to be well received in order to maximize the chances it will be approved. So it is only sensible to make the plan as appealing as you can for your audience. This is one of the most basic marketing lessons: Delight the customer.

So if the people to whom you are presenting like presentations, then prepare a presentation. If they like to read documents, write a document. If they like everything on purple paper, put it on purple paper. The format doesn't really matter; the ideas and substance do.

That said, do not rush out and create a long, traditional marketing plan simply because you believe that is what people want to see. It is worth clarifying the expectations. In most cases, what people really care about are the recommendations and the support.

If your audience really does request a long, traditional plan, I would create a tight, focused plan followed by a detailed appendix. I suspect you won't use the appendix, and next time you will be able to drop it entirely.

A particularly principled person might argue that, no, if a short plan is best, then a short plan should be created and presented, regardless of the wishes of the audience. This is intellectually brave but practically foolish. My advice is to stand on principle and take a risk when the issue is critically important. Taking a huge political risk on a marketing plan doesn't make a lot of sense. Providing a short plan followed by a longer appendix accomplishes both goals.

SHOULDN'T THE CUSTOMER DRIVE THE MARKETING PLAN?

Customers are important. Indeed, it's hard to argue that customers aren't the most important aspect of any business; if you don't have customers, you don't have a business. Delighting customers is a very good way to build a business.

However, customers should not drive the marketing plan. The goal of a business is not just to give customers what they want. The goal is to build long-term profitability. Giving customers what they want is an important way to achieve the goal, but it isn't a goal in and of itself.

In truth, delighting customers and building a great business are different things. Ideally, a business is able to both create happy customers and generate profits in the process. This is the ideal situation.

But it is very possible to delight customers and destroy a business in the process. For example, customers almost always want more features and lower prices; cutting prices while adding more features, however, is rarely a way to build profits over time.

As a result, although it is essential to understand customers in order to create a great plan, the plan cannot be all about the customer. Businesses need to think about how they can profitably meet and shape customer needs to provide more value than their competition. Jeff Immelt, CEO of General Electric, explained the situation well in a recent interview. He noted, "I've spent my lifetime working with customers, and I love customers. I get great insights from them—but I would never let them set our strategy for us. But by talking to them, I can put it in my own language. Customers always pay our bills. But they will never pick our people or set our strategies."[4]

WHO SHOULD WRITE THE MARKETING PLAN?

Marketing plans should be written by the people responsible for actually implementing the plan and delivering the results. This means that a marketing plan should generally be created and owned by whoever is accountable for the results.

Curiously, this means that the marketing department will not always be responsible for creating the marketing plan. In some organizations, the marketing department is primarily focused on communications; the marketing team develops the sales materials and the advertising but is not responsible for the overall business performance and has limited impact on decisions regarding pricing, products, and research. In this case, the marketing team should have input on the plan but should not ultimately create it and own it. Instead, the general manager should create the marketing plan and take responsibility for the results.

A good marketing plan focuses on all aspects of the business, not just on the communications. As a result, it should be created by the people who are responsible for all aspects of the business. In some cases, the general manager is a marketing executive. In other cases, the general manager has a background in sales or operations or finance. In every case, however, the general manager has to understand and believe in the plan. The person on the hook for delivering the profit numbers will ultimately call the shots on the business.

Marketing plans should be written by individuals who know the business well and can think through the best plan. Because the marketing plan plays a critical role in the long-term success of a business, it requires the attention of senior executives.

Delegating the plan to a junior person, or an outside agency, is not a wise approach. Unfortunately, this is exactly what happens at many companies. Very often, those least capable of developing powerful strategies—the junior people—are the ones charged with developing them. Eli Lilly's Michael McGrath notes that at many companies, the person creating the marketing plan "tends to be the associate right out of business school because no one else wants to do it."

WHAT ROLE SHOULD THE CHIEF MARKETING OFFICER PLAY?

The chief marketing officer should be deeply involved in the development of marketing plans. Indeed, one of the primary tools a CMO can use to foster a marketing mindset in a company is to champion and support a marketing planning process; this elevates the discussion of marketing and gets people focused on how marketing can build the business.

However, the CMO should not actually create and write the plan unless she is the general manager and owns the P&L. Having the CMO write the marketing plan seems like an obvious decision because the CMO is the head of, well, marketing. Often, though, the CMO is the wrong person to write the plan, because, usually, the CMO doesn't have responsibility for the business results. In many companies, the CMO plays a functional role, reporting to the CEO and serving as a marketing advisor across the company. In this situation, the CMO should not create the marketing plan because the CMO doesn't own the P&L.

At Procter & Gamble, for example, Jim Stengel had no direct profit responsibility when he was chief marketing officer; the people responsible for delivering the profit numbers worked in the operating divisions. In this case, Stengel should not have been developing marketing plans. He was not accountable for the results, so he should not be writing the plan.

The marketing plans should be created by the business teams. The CMO should have input into the plans, certainly, but ultimately the plan is the responsibility of the team responsible for driving the overall business results.

SHOULDN'T EVERY MARKETING PLAN INCLUDE A SWOT ANALYSIS?

A SWOT analysis (a review of an organization's strengths, weaknesses, opportunities, and threats) is not a required part of a marketing plan, and most marketing plans would be better without it.

A SWOT analysis is a useful tool for understanding a business and the situation ahead. In general, though, a SWOT analysis, though it can help shape the plan, ideally should not appear in the final document.

SWOT analyses have several problems that make them more appropriate for analysis than for the actual plan. First, a SWOT analysis simply organizes and reviews the current state of affairs. It doesn't say anything about what should be done; the implications often are not obvious, and the link to the ensuing plan is tenuous at best. A SWOT analysis certainly isn't a plan. It is also a weak tool for supporting a plan; the information in a SWOT analysis generally can be presented in a far more powerful manner as part of a broader story.

As AspireUp's Roland Jacobs explained, "The SWOT analysis is just a repository of thoughts about the business." Another marketing executive was even more direct when discussing the SWOT, noting, "If I see a SWOT analysis in a marketing plan, I am actually more nervous that they have no plan."

IS THERE A DIFFERENCE BETWEEN A GOAL AND AN OBJECTIVE?

My advice is to use the terms interchangeably.

Some people draw a distinction between goals and objectives, so one page of a marketing plan will show the goals and another page will show the objectives. I think this is just too confusing; it isn't obvious to many people how these things are different. To keep things simple, ignore the distinction.

The spirit is the same whether you use the word *goal* or *objective*: What is the business trying to achieve over the next year?

DOES AN ORGANIZATION NEED A MARKETING PLAN PROCESS?

Every organization should develop marketing plans, and every organization needs a marketing plan process. Without a process—deliverables and deadlines—for creating, reviewing, and monitoring plans, few people will actually create a plan.

Some organizations have incredibly long and detailed marketing plan processes. For example, the marketing plan process at one company I worked with required six pages to summarize. The process kicked off every year in January and ended with approved plans in November. It was a complicated, elaborate, global affair.

A marketing plan process doesn't need to be long, complex, and drawn out. Although some organizations inevitably will end up with a complicated system simply because the organization is enormous and complicated, this is not essential. A marketing plan process can be very simple with just a few critical steps.

Whether simple or complex, every organization needs to have a logical process and timeline for creating a plan. Otherwise, nothing will happen.

Ideally, the marketing plan process is created and owned by the senior management team. The chief executive officer or chief operating officer should be deeply involved in the process. Marketing is essential for business success, so a CEO or COO ultimately should drive and own the process.

If senior management doesn't establish a planning process, it is up to the business or marketing leaders to create one.

WHAT DOES A GOOD PLANNING PROCESS LOOK LIKE?

Great marketing plan processes have several common characteristics; these hold true whether the process is short or long, simple or complicated, focused or thorough.

First, the process must encourage cross-functional participation. A marketing plan that involves only the marketing department will fail to have a big impact on an organization; the plan has to be cross-functional, involving R&D, sales, operations, finance, and perhaps human resources. A marketing plan is different from an operations plan; marketing is not simply another function. Marketing touches everything an organization does to meet customer needs profitably. Treating marketing as a function dooms an organization.

Second, an effective planning process must be focused on the recommendations: the goals or objectives, strategies, and tactics. A process that encourages people to analyze a business without forcing them to identify implications and recommendations will do more harm than good. The focus must be on action.

Third, the planning process ultimately must produce decisions. The reason to write a marketing plan is to set the direction for the business. This involves making decisions. A good planning process, then, will focus on key decision points. The process should have a defined endpoint when the team gets a green light and can move ahead with execution.

Fourth, a marketing plan process needs an owner and champion. A process without a clear leader will not take root; someone needs to drive it forward, setting the dates and clarifying the deliverables.

Finally, the planning process needs senior management support. Ultimately, the priorities of an organization are driven from the top. As a result, the best marketing plan processes are supported by the CEO. It is impractical and unrealistic for the CEO to review the marketing plan for every product, but he or she should be certain that plans are being created, should highlight the importance of the plans, and should review the plans for key products and divisions.

Speed is not a characteristic of great marketing plans, for the simple reason that developing a great plan takes time. A plan assembled in a hurry often ends up being a copy of the prior year's plan; people merely update the charts. This doesn't add much of value. It is far better to take the time and effort required to do a good job. As Malcolm McDonald wrote in his book *Marketing Plans*, "Producing an effective marketing plan that will give your organization competitive advantage is not easy. It takes knowledge, skills, intellect, creativity, and, above all, time."[5]

One marketer described how his company rolled out a new planning process that every business unit was expected to finish in a matter of weeks. As you might expect, the new process failed because there just wasn't enough time to flesh out the strategy. He explained what happened: "There wasn't enough time for critical thinking. It became 'We have to fill out the template.' It ended up being an unbridled mess."

A marketing plan process should take the time required to address the issues facing the business and present a credible plan for the future.

HOW MUCH SHOULD A MARKETING PLAN CHANGE FROM YEAR TO YEAR?

Strategic initiatives and tactics should evolve over time; it would be odd if the tactics for a business were the same every year. The positioning of a business should be consistent, but the initiatives should change. Indeed, if you find that the initiatives in a plan are not changing at all, it is important to ask why this is the case. It usually is not a good sign.

One day in early September 2000 I decided to clean out the files in my office. At the time I was a senior category business director at Kraft Foods, responsible for running a collection of brands with annual sales of more than $500 million. I had recently moved into the role and in the process had changed offices, moving into my predecessor's office.

So I set aside some time and started opening up the cabinets. They were full of papers and reports and documents—and about a decade's worth of marketing plans.

I cracked open the marketing plan for 1993, an enormous document that described a challenging business situation and identified issues that had to be addressed. I then opened the marketing plan for 1994. Although the pages were different, the theme was the same; the plan described the same challenging business situation and identified the same issues that needed to be addressed. I then opened the plan from 1995 and read about the same thing. It went on and on. The marketing plans were all different but all essentially the same. The situation hadn't changed substantially.

Each marketing plan, however, was long and detailed and thorough. It was clear that a talented team of people had spent weeks creating the plans.

Unfortunately, nothing happened and nothing changed; the same plan could have been presented in any year. The entire exercise was a waste of time.

A marketing plan should be a living document, changing to reflect the situation facing a business. A static marketing plan indicates a lack of creativity (no new ideas) or a lack of effectiveness (no progress), or both.

HOW IS A MARKETING PLAN DIFFERENT FROM A BUSINESS PLAN?

Marketing plans are similar to business plans; both documents set the course and highlight how the business will deliver sales and profits over time.

The documents are different in that business plans generally include many more topics, including operations strategy, financing issues, and human resource issues. Marketing is just one topic within a business plan.

To an extent, a good marketing plan provides the driving theme for a business plan. The marketing plan provides the spark and the big picture. The business plan includes all the functional activities that need to occur to keep the entire organization moving ahead.

ISN'T A LONG MARKETING PLAN A SIGN OF A SAVVY MARKETER?

Smart marketers do not create long marketing plans. Indeed, the reverse is true; people who are gifted at marketing produce tight, focused, compelling marketing plans.

To an extent, the size of a marketing plan reflects the level of marketing savvy of an organization. A company that doesn't understand and value marketing might not have a marketing plan at all. If there is a formal plan, it will probably be very superficial because nobody spends much time on it and nobody cares about it very much.

As a company becomes more marketing focused, marketing plans tend to get longer and more thorough; the business team uncovers more information and data and includes that information in the plan. Indeed, some of the longest and most ineffective marketing plans are created by organizations that realize marketing is important but have yet to understand and apply the insight that knowing things about your customer does not lead to better results; you have to actually do something with the information.

Companies that are extremely savvy often have very tight, refined marketing plans. The organization understands that focus is essential and that it isn't how much people know that's important; it's what they actually do that matters. Procter & Gamble, for example, is one of the leading marketing companies in the world. Marketing teams at P&G routinely produce very short, focused marketing plans of about six pages. Stephen Cunliffe, president of Nestlé's frozen foods division, presents marketing plans for his billion-dollar organization in twenty pages.

DO I REALLY HAVE TO KNOW HOW TO WRITE A GOOD PLAN?

The honest answer is no, you don't have to know how to write a great marketing plan. You don't have to pass an exam to write a marketing plan. The local police won't be after you if you keep writing long, traditional, and ineffective plans. The American Marketing Association doesn't issue citations for poor plans. Indeed, in some organizations you will be very safe sticking with the usual approach.

However, very few things can help your career more than learning how to create a great marketing plan. This is true for several reasons.

First, great marketing plans are very often approved. As a result, creating a good marketing plan means you will have the opportunity to actually implement your ideas. Because results ultimately matter most, it is essential to have the opportunity to put your ideas into practice. Coming up with great ideas that never get implemented is frustrating; you have to actually do something to have an impact.

Second, in most organizations, marketing plans are very visible. Marketing plans are generally reviewed by very senior executives. As a result, marketers who develop tight, focused, and compelling plans simply look smarter and more capable than executives who develop weak plans. As every marketing executive knows, perceptions matter most; being known as a smart, savvy leader is a very good thing.

David Hirschler has spent years leading brands at Colgate and Liz Claiborne. He observed that the people who create strong marketing plans stand out in an organization. According to Hirschler, "If you're really good at it, it's going to say good things about you." Similarly, executives who develop confused plans that lack focus inevitably look bad. Hirschler continued, "You can be a great marketer, but if you have a muddled presentation you aren't going to be well regarded."

Third, marketing plans can be time consuming, so executives who are efficient at writing them get more done. People who struggle to write plans end up having to devote far more time to the task. Being able to construct a strong plan in a relatively short period of time is a competitive advantage among peers at a similar level.

It is difficult for a tennis player to win a match if he can't serve well. The serve in tennis is an essential, core skill; it starts the game. A good serve doesn't guarantee that a player will win the match, but a terrible serve virtually guarantees a loss.

Similarly, it is very difficult for a marketer to be successful if she can't create a good marketing plan. Creating powerful marketing plans is a core skill. The ability to create a good plan doesn't guarantee success, but a bad plan, or no plan, virtually guarantees less than optimal results.

ISN'T THIS ALL PRETTY OBVIOUS?

It is indeed. The core ideas presented in this book are not revolutionary: create a plan, be clear on your objectives, focus on a few important strategic initiatives, and provide compelling support for your recommendation. As marketer Greg Wozniak noted, "It's almost scary how basic it is. It sounds almost too basic."

Of course, the fact that the basic concepts are simple doesn't mean that they aren't useful. Harvard professor Clayton Christensen observed in his book *The Innovator's Dilemma*, "I have found that many of life's most useful insights are often quite simple."[6]

Simple or not, the reality is that many companies create marketing plans that are a disaster; they are too long, too complicated, and too focused on random facts. The plan and the big ideas are obscured by the weight of the data and somewhat irrelevant pieces of information.

Sergio Pereira summarized the situation well, explaining, "So much of marketing is common sense, but it all goes away when you write marketing plans."

Chapter 12

EXAMPLE: FLAHAVAN'S

THE MARKETING PLAN BELOW IS A hypothetical plan written for Flahavan's, an Irish food company.

Flahavan & Sons is an old, well-established company in Ireland. It dates back to the 1700s, when an oats mill, powered by the nearby Mahon River, was built in Kilmacthomas, Ireland. Now in its sixth generation of family ownership, Flahavan's is Ireland's oldest family-owned food company.

Flahavan's is the leading brand of porridge in Ireland, with more than 50 percent of the total market. The company makes products only under the Flahavan's brand, operating as a branded house. Virtually all of Flahavan's sales are from the Irish market; the company has a limited presence in other countries.

The marketing plan that follows is one that Flahavan's might develop, written in a presentation format. I have changed all the specific information to maintain confidentiality. The plan is short, focused, and action oriented. It is simple, as marketing plans should be. It also includes support for all the key recommendations. It is a good model to follow.

* * *

Exhibit 12.1   Marketing Plan Example

2013 Marketing Plan
Flahavan's

This plan is purely an example. The data, people and strategies discussed in this plan are all illustrative.

Kyle Malley, Patricia O'Connor, and Seamus Hanlon
October 15, 2012
Dublin, Ireland

Agenda

1. Executive Summary
2. State of the Business
3. Goals/Objectives
4. Strategic Initiatives
5. Tactics
6. Financial Implications
7. Risks and Contingencies
8. Milestones
9. Summary

Flahavan's is poised for further growth

- Flahavan's has delivered strong results, with 2012 profits up +8%, due to robust category growth and a modest price increase

- Flahavan's has two goals for 2013: increase profit by +9% and maintain share of the porridge category at 62.1%

- The 2013 marketing plan is focused on three big initiatives
  - Continue to drive category growth by promoting health benefits
  - Launch quick oats portable cups to address growing need for convenience and build margins
  - Evaluate new snacking line and expansion into U.S. market

- The primary risk facing the business is that product costs may increase more than expected. If this occurs we will increase list prices to maintain margins

---

Agenda

1. Executive Summary
2. State of the Business
3. Goals/Objectives
4. Strategic Initiatives
5. Tactics
6. Financial Implications
7. Risks and Contingencies
8. Milestones
9. Summary

Flahavan's Positioning and Vision

- Vision:

> We will be the leader in Oat-Based Products

- Positioning:

To busy, active women in Ireland, Flahavan's is the brand of breakfast food
that is most nutritious because Flahavan's is natural and high in fiber and has
a low glycaemic index

2012 will be an excellent year for Flahavan's

- The Flahavan's business is performing well across all measures

  - 2012 sales volume will be up by +4% with revenues up +6%
  - Profits will finish the year up +8%
  - Volume share will be up +0.8 points to 62.1%

- Strong results are due to category growth, a price increase, and reduced competitive activity

  - The porridge category is forecast to grow by +3% this year due to an increased focus on nutrition among consumers
  - Our +2.5% list price increase contributed to revenue and profit growth and allowed us to increase advertising by +11%
  - O'Briens, our key competitor, followed our price increase and reduced marketing spending in an apparent bid to boost short-term profits

The challenge for Flahavan's is to drive continued category growth

- The porridge category has grown by an average of +4% in volume over the last five years. This growth has been the primary profit driver for our business

- However, there is evidence that category growth is beginning to slow

Irish Porridge Category
Volume Change

2009	+6%
2010	+6%
2011	+4%
2012 Forecast	+3%
2012 1Half	+4%
2012 2Half Forecast	+1%

- Maintaining category growth is critical for continued profit growth in the business

---

Agenda

Flahavan's is focused on driving strong profit growth in 2013 while maintaining share

2013 Objectives

1. Increase profits by +9%

2. Maintain market share at 62.1%

Flahavan's Results

	Profit Change	Share
2010	+2%	60.8%
2011	+4%	61.3%
2012 Forecast	+8%	62.1%
2013 Objective	+9%	62.1%

Agenda

1. Executive Summary
2. State of the Business
3. Goals/Objectives
4. Strategic Initiatives
5. Tactics
6. Financial Implications
7. Risks and Contingencies
8. Milestones
9. Summary

To drive growth in 2013, the business will focus on three strategic initiatives

Strategic Initiatives

1. Continue to drive category growth by promoting health benefits

2. Launch quick oats portable cups to address growing need for convenience and build margins

3. Evaluate new snacking line and expansion into U.S. market

Promoting the category is essential

- There is an opportunity to further grow the category

  - Only 48% of households currently serve porridge
  - Porridge makes up only 41% of breakfasts in households that serve porridge

- Health is the main opportunity for driving additional category growth

  - Health concerns are increasing
  - There is limited awareness of the health benefits of porridge

% of Irish Women

	2007	2008	2009	2010
Concerned about Health	42%	48%	47%	52%
Aware of Health Benefit of Porridge	31%	38%	39%	41%

Launching portable cups will address convenience and build margins

- Convenience is a significant issue in the category

    - The #1 reason people do not eat porridge in the morning is convenience, or lack of time
    - Convenience will likely become more important for our consumers going forward due to increases in dual-income households

- Quick oats portable cups addresses convenience need

    - Portable cups product is simple to prepare: just add hot water
    - Concept received strong concept and product test scores
    - 61% of consumers agreed the product was more convenient

- Margins on quick oats cups are higher than our traditional progress oatlets 1kg pack

Exploring longer-term growth opportunities is critical

- Our business is currently reliant on one category. Slowing category growth or increased competition will impact overall growth rates

- Snacking is a compelling growth opportunity

    - Huge and growing market
    - A logical extension for our business
    - A good fit for our health positioning

- The U.S. market warrants consideration

    - An enormous opportunity: over $1 billion in revenue
    - A growing market
    - Lots of potential: similar-sized companies have been able to launch successful niche products

Agenda

1. Executive Summary
2. State of the Business
3. Goals/Objectives
4. Strategic Initiatives
5. Tactics
6. Financial Implications
7. Risks and Contingencies
8. Milestones
9. Summary

To drive the category we will expand advertising and PR programs

- Advertising has proven to be effective at growing the category
  - The category grows significantly faster when we advertise

- PR is a major opportunity to expand awareness of health benefits
  - 2012 efforts have generated 42 major news stories about health benefits of the category

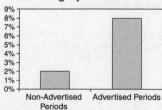

Category Growth

The 2013 plan includes a launch of portable cups in the second quarter

- Announce product line in first quarter with a second-quarter start ship

- Launch a three-item line: original, strawberry, brown sugar

  - Ensure substantial shelf presence
  - Provide variety for consumers

- Support heavily

  - Build awareness through advertising in second and third quarters
  - Drive trial with sampling program and in-store coupons
  - Cross-sell new products on existing items

To explore growth opportunities we will invest in innovation

- Create a snack innovation team

  - Hire an innovation manager
  - Complete snacking market structure study
  - Identify promising concepts and put into test

- Begin exploration of the U.S. market

  - Identify outside consulting firm to develop a recommendation
  - Validate firm's analysis and create launch team if appropriate

Flahavan's 2013 Marketing Plan Summary

Goals/Objectives

Primary Objective

Increase profit by +9%

Secondary Objective

Maintain share at 62.1%

Strategic Initiatives

Drive category growth by promoting health benefits

Launch quick oats portable cups

Explore growth opportunities

Tactics

- Expand advertising program
- Increase PR program to secure media attention

- Launch three-item line in Q2
- Support with advertising
- Drive trial with sampling, coupons

- Create snack innovation team
- Hire consulting firm to develop recommendation

Agenda

1. Executive Summary
2. State of the Business
3. Goals/Objectives
4. Strategic Initiatives
5. Tactics
6. Financial Implications
7. Risks and Contingencies
8. Milestones
9. Summary

Building category and new cup line will require additional spending

- Increasing the category will require sharp increase in media and PR spending

- New cup line will require advertising and promotional support

- Product costs are expected to be up slightly

	2012	2013	Change	
Category Growth	+3%	+5%	+2 pts	Up due to category build initiative
Flahavan's Share	62.1%	62.1%	--	Flat share
Flahavan's Volume (MM kgs)	50.0	52.5	+5%	Growing due to category expansion
Flahavan's Revenue	30.0	32.1	+7%	Up due to higher price cup products
Flahavan's Advertising	3.5	4.3	+22%	Up to support programs
Flahavan's Promotions	1.2	1.5	+29%	Up due to new products and PR
Flahavan's Profit	5.4	5.9	+9%	

Agenda

1. Executive Summary
2. State of the Business
3. Goals/Objectives
4. Strategic Initiatives
5. Tactics
6. Financial Implications
7. Risks and Contingencies
8. Milestones
9. Summary

<u>The main risk facing the business is product cost</u>

<u>Risks</u>

1. Sharp rise in product costs
   -Plan anticipates a 2.5% increase
   -Commodity costs have been volatile

2. Increased promotional activity from competitors

3. Category building efforts are unsuccessful

<u>Contingencies</u>

Lead a list price increase if required to achieve plan

Spend back part 50% of the price increase to further support category

Shift advertising creative from category building to differentiation

Develop new creative to ensure strong communication

<u>Agenda</u>

1. Executive Summary
2. State of the Business
3. Goals/Objectives
4. Strategic Initiatives
5. Tactics
6. Financial Implications
7. <u>Risks and Contingencies</u>
8. Milestones
9. Summary

Milestones

Milestone	Date
Complete category building creative	March 31
Receive advertising test scores	April 15
Gain distribution for portable cups line at all key retailers	May 15
Achieve 40% unaided awareness for portable cups line	July 15
Complete snacking structure study	June 1
Receive report on U.S. opportunity	July 15

Flahavan's is poised for further growth

- Flahavan's has delivered strong results, with 2012 profits up +8%, due to robust category growth and a modest price increase

- Flahavan's has two goals for 2013: increase profit by +9% and maintain share of the porridge category at 62.1%

- The 2013 marketing plan is focused on three big initiatives
  - Continue to drive category growth by promoting health benefits
  - Launch quick oats portable cups to address growing need for convenience and build margins
  - Evaluate new snacking line and expansion into U.S. market

- The primary risk facing the business is that product costs may increase more than expected. If this occurs we will increase list prices to maintain margins

Chapter 13

EXAMPLE: EDZO'S

THIS IS AN ILLUSTRATIVE MARKETING PLAN for Edzo's, a small restaurant in Evanston, Illinois. It was written by five MBA students as part of my marketing strategy course at the Kellogg School of Management: Ryan Farnan, Matt Fitzgerald, Matt Hanculak, Matt House, and Chris Reynolds.

Edzo's Burger Shop is a premium, independent, quick-serve hamburger restaurant. Store owner Eddie Lakin, nicknamed Edzo, estimates that he sells between three hundred and five hundred burgers per day. The shop is open Tuesday through Sunday from 10:30 a.m. to 4:00 p.m. Edzo is the face of the brand, and he operates the cash register daily.

* * *

Marketing Plan: Edzo's Burger Shop
Rare Initiatives, Well Done
December 6, 2011

EXECUTIVE SUMMARY

Edzo's Burger Shop is struggling. Revenue has fallen 20 percent in the last year as competitors, especially Five Guys, have stolen market share. Not surprisingly, the revenue decline has had a major impact on profitability.

This marketing plan is focused on rebuilding profits. The goal is to increase profit by 50 percent over the next year with a focus on three strategic initiatives: raising prices, building the store experience, and increasing buying rate.

STATE OF THE BUSINESS

Edzo's Burger Shop is a specialty burger eatery that offers the classic American meal: a hamburger, fries, and a milk shake.

POSITIONING

Critics and diners alike deem Edzo's the highest-quality quick-serve burger shop in Evanston because of its impeccable ingredients and unrivaled freshness. Edzo's grinds its meat daily, it never freezes its meat, it hand cuts its fries daily, it double fries its fries so they are crispy, and it cooks the burgers to order. Furthermore, it works with local farms to provide the highest-quality beef. No other outlet provides such quality and freshness.

Edzo's targets burger enthusiasts who prioritize freshness and quality. Macro food trends such as local, organic, humane, sustainable, antibiotic-free, and grass-fed carry considerable weight with this target. What's more, they value quality measures like grinding the meat daily and cooking it to order. Edzo's does not target calorie counters.

Edzo's positioning is clear: For burger connoisseurs, Edzo's is the brand of burger shop that provides the highest-quality burger experience because of its premium, fresh ingredients and exceptional preparation.

RECENT RESULTS

Despite its premium positioning, nearly unanimous positive reviews, and strong word of mouth, Edzo's business has decreased 20 percent over the last year.

The primary reason for this decline was the opening of a popular Five Guys Burgers & Fries franchise nearby in October 2010. Five Guys occupies a niche area in the quick-serve market focused on quality. It provides premium pricing. It does not cook its burgers to order, and it offers a more limited selection of fries. It is the closest option to Edzo's in the competitive set.

A secondary factor is sustained competition from a crowded marketplace. Direct competitors include other quick-serve burger eateries such as Neü Über Bürger and Burger King. Indirect competitors include premium quick-serve eateries such as Chipotle, Panera Bread, and Potbelly Sandwich Works.

When analyzing possible growth strategies, a major constraint for Edzo's is its limited hours. Owner Eddie Lakin, an internationally trained chef, has made being home with family each night his top priority, and thus the eatery is only open from 10:30 a.m. to 4:00 p.m. Tuesday through Sunday. Though limited hours reduce revenue potential, Lakin is insistent on the current operating structure. Therefore, our proposed business strategies are focused around maximizing the existing lunchtime business through unrelenting focus on the quality of the Edzo's burger experience.

Despite the limited operating schedule, Edzo's generated strong estimated yearly revenues of $979,200 and profits of about $275,000 from October 2009 to October 2010. This profitability was fueled by high volumes of burgers and high margins on complementary items. But since Five Guys opened in October 2010, Edzo's has lost approximately 20 percent of its revenues, falling to $806,400, with profits of just over $172,000. In the process, Edzo's lost a quarter of its net margin, which fell from 28 percent to 21 percent.

GOALS/OBJECTIVES

Given the current state of the Evanston market and the current financial state of the business, we believe that Edzo's should set an aggressive but attainable goal of increasing profits by 50 percent in the next twelve months.

STRATEGIC INITIATIVES

To achieve these goals, we recommend that Edzo's implement three strategic initiatives: increase prices, build the in-store experience, and increase buying rate.

STRATEGIC INITIATIVE 1: INCREASE PRICES

Edzo's current pricing structure neither reflects nor takes advantage of its value proposition. Edzo's closest competitor, Five Guys, offers a 6.6-ounce two-patty hamburger with no cheese for $5.39, or about $0.82 per ounce. By comparison, Edzo's also charges $5.39 for its "Double," also a two-patty hamburger with no cheese. However, Edzo's Double is 8.0 ounces, or about $0.67 per ounce. Edzo's is offering more burger for less money, both in terms of size and gourmet preparation. Increased prices on specific menu items can both instantly increase profits and help to better position the restaurant as a premium burger experience.

Edzo's should increase its prices on all four of its burgers to just under the nearest whole dollar, maintaining the first digit of each price point to preserve psychological pricing. This translates into a forty-cent increase on the Single, a sixty-cent increase on the Double, a seventy-cent increase on the Triple, and a twenty-cent increase on the Char Burger.

Exhibit 13.1 Proposed Price Increases

	Current Price	Proposed Price	Dollar Increase	Percentage Increase
Single	$3.59	$3.99	$0.40	11.1%
Double	5.39	5.99	0.60	11.1%
Triple	7.29	7.99	0.70	9.6%
Char Burger	5.79	5.99	0.20	3.5%

These price increases address the two issues outlined above. First, and most important, they differentiate Edzo's from competitors by signaling the premium nature of the Edzo's burger experience. Second, they will increase profits as discussed in the Financial Implications section below. From a customer perspective, the proposed price increases are likely to go unnoticed by all except the most frequent Edzo's customers. Further, regular customers who value the Edzo's experience will be unlikely to change their purchasing habits given that the overall scope of the price increase is relatively small, both in dollar and percentage terms.

STRATEGIC INITIATIVE 2: BUILD IN-STORE EXPERIENCE

Edzo's offers a unique hamburger experience that standardized chain establishments and low-quality efficiency shops cannot match. The eatery possesses unrivaled quality in its product offering and a distinctive in-store experience, but there is ample room to create further differentiation in these areas. Currently, Edzo's marketing communications are not clear enough in establishing its points of difference vis-à-vis its competitors. The company can earn more business and loyalty through customer reinforcement of its best qualities.

Tactic 1: Ensure That All In-Store Communication Articulates
Edzo's Positioning around Freshness and High Quality

Edzo's daily beef grinding is a major element of its product quality. Furthermore, Edzo's beef is never frozen, it is locally sourced from small farmers in Illinois who practice sustainable farming methods, and it is cooked to order. Five Guys and Burger King do not offer this quality. These differentiated elements of freshness and quality are at the heart of Edzo's positioning.

Edzo's must highlight and brand these qualities across all viable elements of the eatery, as Chipotle has done very successfully by branding its napkins, counters, and signage with ingredient stories. Edzo's must similarly highlight its taste advantage created by the superior quality of its ingredients and preparation. A pertinent example would be an "Edzo's: Freshly Ground Today" sticker placed on the packaging of all burgers, in order to make a powerful, relevant brand statement at minimal cost. By creating a story around the quality of the ingredients and making that story prominent across its store space and distributed items, Edzo's will create a sticky, hard-to-replicate connection between its product and its consumers.

Tactic 2: Discontinue Delivery Service

Delivery is antithetical to Edzo's value proposition, in that it jeopardizes quality and pulls away from the unique store experience. The quality of the product suffers in the delivery process because the burgers and fries steam in the bag, and thus customers are likely to receive soggy and lukewarm food items that have been stripped of the Edzo's premium during the lengthy delivery process. *New York Times* food critic Peter Meehan has commented, "These are burgers to be eaten on premises"—and they should be whenever possible. On-premises customers are engulfed by the tastes and aromas that make Edzo's products unique treats, and they are surrounded by messaging that will solidify positive brand associations and keep them coming back. Discontinuing delivery will focus Edzo's attention on its in-store experience, further enhancing the dining experience for customers.

Tactic 3: Create a Second Line for Faster Ordering

Edzo's should create a second line with a scaled-down menu to expedite the ordering process. This will shorten the wait time in the primary line, improving the consumer in-store experience and decreasing the likelihood of line abandonment, which can be destructive to profits at such a highly trafficked venue. This measure will also help Edzo's handle increased volume during peak hours and potentially lead to greater repeat business from time-constrained local fans who require speed as a complement to quality. This new line is quite distinct from delivery, as it requires customers to physically enter the store (albeit in an expedited manner) and gets food in their hands at the peak of freshness. By adding operational efficiency and improving the customer experience without sacrificing quality or store character, this new line will be a profit-accretive improvement that stays loyal to the brand's image.

STRATEGIC INITIATIVE 3: INCREASE BUYING RATE

Edzo's does not struggle in creating trial; more challenging is sustaining a steady buying rate from its consumers. Edzo estimates the average customer purchases from the store slightly more than once a month. As shown in exhibit 13.2, by increasing the monthly buying rate by between 10 and 20 percent, Edzo can increase daily visits by between twenty-three and forty-six customers. The financial ramifications of this increase are explored further later in this document.

Tactic 1: Create a Loyalty Program Centered on
a Once-per-Month Dinner Event

To build buying rate among repeat consumers, Edzo can offer a special dining event for any customer who buys from the store at least four times in a month. Once a month on a weekday evening, Edzo can host special burger events, cooking demonstrations, or offer a special off-menu premium item (e.g., a Wagyu beef burger). Customers who have received at least four marks on their monthly punch card will be admitted to the event. The event will not be provided free of charge to customers but will foster a sense of exclusivity for these loyal patrons, build excitement by offering something new from Edzo's, and offer an extra source of revenue for Edzo, while not requiring him to change his daily hours.

Tactic 2: Drive Additional Usage with Off-Peak Promotions

Though Edzo's is only open from 10:30 a.m. to 4:00 p.m., business slows dramatically after 3 p.m. Driving purchase during this slow pre-dinner period would certainly serve Edzo's sales growth. Between 3:00 p.m. and 4:00 p.m., Edzo's should offer a special promotion to its Facebook fans on side items like French fries, milk shakes, and

Exhibit 13.2   Repeat Analysis

Total visits per month	8,400
Average visit per customer	1.5
Customers per month	5,600
Impact of 10% additional repeat on monthly visits	560
Impact of 10% additional repeat on daily visits	23

drinks—"$1 fries with purchase," "$2 shake with purchase of two burgers," etc. If consumers see the Facebook post and mention the special code word for that day's promotion, they'll receive the deal. As the deals are only offered to Edzo's Facebook fans, this tactic will specifically drive repeat purchase from existing consumers.

Tactic #3: Utilize Existing Web Properties to Keep Edzo's Top of Mind with Customers

Edzo's currently utilizes a mix of digital platforms to communicate with customers: Twitter, Facebook, a website, and a blog. Unfortunately, not all platforms are maintained on a regular basis. Each has the ability to deliver Edzo's positioning, but in slightly different ways. To simplify and amplify his message, Edzo should focus primarily on Facebook and discontinue his blog and Twitter feed. The ultimate goal is to keep Edzo's top of mind, especially against competitors Five Guys and Burger King.

Facebook: Edzo's Facebook page offers a plethora of information, but it must become the primary means by which he communicates the company's positioning with loyal fans—photos, live updates, news articles, reviews, and the like to communicate the current state of marketing activity. As mentioned before, Facebook can also be a means of distributing promotions to loyal fans utilizing special code words. Edzo should plan on engaging with his Facebook audience at least once a day, and give them a special offer at least once per week.

Website: The website must showcase Edzo's positioning of quality and freshness. All reviews and television appearances should be archived in an easy-to-retrieve structure. While the website might be more static than a Facebook page (or a way to simply communicate info), it must clearly explain Edzo's freshness and quality positioning.

FINANCIAL IMPLICATIONS

Prior to the entry of Five Guys, Edzo's was averaging approximately 425 customers per day, earning annual profits of about $275,000 on revenues of just over $975,000, as shown in exhibit 13.3. With the

Exhibit 13.3 P&L Estimate

	Before Five Guys	After Five Guys
Burgers per day	425	350
Average check	$8.00	$8.00
Variable cost per check	3.25	3.25
Annual P&L		
Revenue	979,200	806,400
COGS	397,800	327,600
Gross margin	581,400	478,800
Labor	138,240	138,240
Facility	120,000	120,000
Maintenance	24,000	24,000
Supplies	12,000	12,000
Other	12,000	12,000
SG&A total	306,240	306,240
Net income	275,160	172,560

entry of Five Guys, Edzo's lost nearly 20 percent of its business, lowering annual revenues and profits to approximately $800,000 and $175,000. This lowered margins significantly, from over 28 percent to just 21 percent, and overall profit fell by nearly 40 percent.

The suggested strategic initiatives of taking price increases as well as increasing repeat business provide two separate levers to increase profits. There are various combinations that will deliver profits of at least $259,000, reaching the targeted 50 percent increase, as shown in exhibit 13.4.

As explored above, it seems reasonable to assume that Edzo's could realistically generate and support between twenty-five and fifty additional visits per day with better repeat business. This would increase total visits per day to between 375 and 400. Along with pricing increases that increase the average sale to between $8.50 and $8.75, Edzo's could easily increase profits to the targeted range. Amounts toward the higher end of both ranges would improve annual profits to nearly $330,000, which represents a 20 percent improvement over the pre-Five Guys period.

Exhibit 13.4   Sensitivity Analysis—Estimated Profit

		Average Check $					
		7.75	8.00	8.25	8.50	8.75	9.00
	325	114,960	138.360	161,760	185,160	208,560	213,960
Visits per Day	350	147,360	172,560	197,760	222,960	248,160	273,360
	375	179,760	206,760	233,760	260,760	287,760	314,760
	400	212,160	240,960	269,760	298,560	327,360	354,160
	425	244,560	275,160	305760	336,360	366,960	397,560
	450	276,960	309,360	341,760	374,160	406,560	438,960

In addition, there is an opportunity to offer promotional events that improve repeat business and improve profits. For instance, if Edzo's implemented a loyalty program and twenty patrons paid a $25 fee to spend "An Evening with Edzo" with a special feature burger of the month, this could generate nearly $5,000 per year in additional profit for the restaurant. The financial benefits of this would extend past the evening itself, of course, because of the additional repeat traffic it would likely generate.

The estimates in exhibit 13.4 do not take into account the cost of any off-peak promotions. It is difficult to estimate the volume of the promotions, and it is assumed that those promotions will be net accretive to the bottom line since the cost of the promotional items (e.g., discounted fries or shake) is far lower than the margin earned on an additional hamburger sale.

RISKS AND CONTINGENCIES

Of the initiatives proposed, increasing prices is the most risky recommendation. Because Edzo's does not have the resources to conduct research into consumer price elasticity, it is unclear what consumers' reaction to price increases will be. Therefore, the implementation of in-store signage around freshness and quality of food is paramount in importance and will give customers the proof that they should be paying more for an Edzo's burger.

The planned increase in business from the above initiatives will be for naught if Edzo's cannot operationally process more customers during peak hours. The length of the line during Edzo's peak operating hours leads to abandonment. With a bevy of lunch and burger options nearby, consumers can still easily get their burger fix. The second line, with a limited take-out menu, should alleviate this, but it remains to be seen if Edzo's can deliver the same quality product in an even more crowded environment at a reasonable or faster pace.

MILESTONES

Edzo's needs to monitor its progress as it seeks to increase its profits by 50 percent over the next twelve months. The following will provide insights into the health of the marketing plan.

Price increase: Track unit sales and average check to determine if pricing increase is effective; this should be measured each month for twelve months, and compared against plan.

Build in-store experience: Track the incremental revenue and utilization rate associated with second line on a monthly basis. Additionally, in order to track the success of the new in-store messaging, Edzo's could track how many Facebook comments and Yelp reviews cite "freshness," or they could casually ask people at the register to do word association with the Edzo's brand name. Although these are not empirically rigorous techniques, they would at least give Edzo's a sense of whether the repositioning has been at all effective.

Buying rate evaluation: To understand if Edzo's is increasing its buying rate among repeat users, it must assess the success of its loyalty program. On a monthly basis, Edzo's can simply track how many people are qualifying for, and participating in, its special dinner events.

Edzo also needs to increase his "likes" on Facebook. He can monitor website traffic to understand how people are using the site. Edzo's should seek to go from 1,189 to 2,000 "likes" within twelve months, and engage with fans or create public posts at least once per day.

CONCLUSION

As a sole proprietor, Edzo primarily measures "success" by his quality of life—he makes a living doing what he loves, and he gets to spend ample time with his family. However, that should not preclude him from implementing some practical strategies to generate growth in his business. Quite simply, we believe a goal of increasing profits by 50 percent over the next twelve months is eminently achievable. Central to attaining this goal is consistent reinforcement of the perception that Edzo's provides the highest-quality burger experience available. This informs our three strategic recommendations for the company: increase prices to drive profitability and enhance the perception of quality; build the in-store experience to consistently communicate the quality of Edzo's ingredients and preparation; and increase the buying rate through tactics that drive the perception that Edzo's is a special restaurant that caters to the most sophisticated burger lover. Following these recommendations will help Edzo ensure that he maintains the quality of life that he has worked hard to achieve, while creating more wealth for himself and his employees.

Exhibit 13.5 Edzo's Marketing Plan Summary

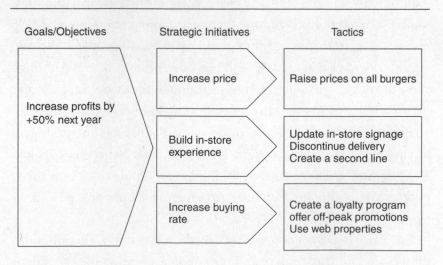

NOTES

1 INTRODUCTION

1. Kathleen Carroll, interview, April 17, 2012.
2. Ibid.

2 WHY BOTHER?

1. Joseph Menn, "HP Bosses Defend Strategy Shift after Shares Fall," *Financial Times*, August 22, 2011, 1.
2. David Goldman, "HP CEO Apotheker Fired, Replaced by Meg Whitman," CNNMoney, August 22, 2011, http://money.cnn.com/2011/09/22/technology/hp_ceo_fired/index.htm, last accessed May 21, 2012.
3. "Marketing 50," *Advertising Age*, November 12, 2007, S-1.
4. Malcolm McDonald, *Marketing Plans*, 5th ed. (Oxford, UK: Butterworth-Heinemann), 13.
5. Intel Corporation, "What Happens in an Internet Minute," http://www.intel.com/content/www/us/en/communications/internet-minute-infographic.html, last accessed May 21, 2012.
6. Richard Siklos, "Made to Measure," *Fortune*, March 3, 2008, 72.
7. Dawn Pickett Leijon, interview, April 23, 2012.
8. Phil Marineau, presentation at Kellogg School of Management, September 15, 2011.
9. Jeff Kehoe, "How to Save Good Ideas," *Harvard Business Review*, October 2010, 130.
10. Michael E. Porter, Jay W. Lorsch, and Nitin Nohria, "Seven Surprises for New CEOs," *Harvard Business Review*, October 2004, 71.
11. Noel Tichy and Ram Charan, "Speed, Simplicity, Self-Confidence: An Interview with Jack Welch," *Harvard Business Review*, September–October 1989, 3.

12. Lynn Lunsford, "New Company, Same Problems for Ford's CEO," *Wall Street Journal*, September 7, 2006, B10.

13. A. G. Lafley, *The Game-Changer: How You Can Drive Revenue and Profit Growth with Innovation* (New York: Crown Business, 2008), 75.

3   THE PROBLEMS

1. Mercedes M. Cardona, "CMOs Under Fire," *Advertising Age*, May 3, 2004, 81.

2. The Latin School of Chicago, *Long Range Plan*, August, 2007, http://www.latinschool.org/ftpimages/348/download/download _group10808_id347640.pdf, last accessed September 8, 2012.

3. *The Economist*, "Future Tense: The Global CMO," 2008, http://grap hics.eiu.com/upload/Google%20Text.pdf, last accessed May 21, 2012.

4. Rajat Gupta and Jim Wendler, "Leading Change: An Interview with the CEO of P&G," *McKinsey Quarterly*, July 2005, http://www .mckinseyquarterly.com/Leading_change_An_interview_with_the _CEO_of_P_G_1648, last accessed May 21, 2012.

5. Noel Tichy and Ram Charan, "Speed, Simplicity, Self-Confidence: An Interview with Jack Welch," *Harvard Business Review*, September– October 1989, 3.

6. Malcolm McDonald, *Marketing Plans*, 5th ed. (Oxford, UK: Butterworth-Heinemann), 31.

7. William M. Luther, *The Marketing Plan*, 3rd ed. (New York: AMACOM, 2001), xiii.

8. McDonald, *Marketing Plans*, 286.

4   THE KEY ELEMENTS

1. Dictionary.com, www.dictionary.com, last accessed May 19, 2012.

2. Development Dimensions International Inc.'s 2005 survey of 4,559 corporate managers in thirty-six countries, as cited in "All Talk?" *Business Week*, March 6, 2006, 13.

3. Thomas A. Stewart and Louise O'Brien, "Execution without Excuses," *Harvard Business Review*, March 2005, 106.

4. Ilan Brat and Bryan Grulet, "Global Trade Galvanizes Caterpillar," *Wall Street Journal*, February 26, 2007, B7.

5. Paul Davies and Joann S. Lublin, "As Crises Pile Up, Bristol CEO Relies on Board Allies," *Wall Street Journal*, July 1, 2005, 1.

6. Malcolm McDonald, *Marketing Plans*, 5th ed. (Oxford, UK: Butterworth-Heinemann), 49.

7. Betsy Morris, "What Makes Apple Golden," *Fortune*, March 17, 2008, 72.

8. Adam Bryant, "Planes, Cars and Cathedrals," *New York Times*, September 6, 2009, 2.

9. Walt Disney 2011 Annual Report, p. 1.
10. UPS 2011 Annual Report, p. 3.
11. Eli Lilly and Company submission to the U.S. Food and Drug Administration, August 10, 2004, 15, http://www.fda.gov/ohrms/dockets/da ilys/04/aug04/082404/04d-0042-c00034-vol3.pdf, last accessed May 21, 2012.

5 THE BEST MARKETING PLANS

1. Thomas A. Stewart and Louise O'Brien, "Execution without Excuses," *Harvard Business Review*, March 2005, 110.
2. "Top 10 Leadership Tips from Jeff Immelt," *Fast Company*, April 2004, 96.
3. James M. Kilts, *Doing What Matters* (New York: Crown Business, 2007), 24.
4. Barry Schwartz, *The Paradox of Choice* (New York: HarperCollins, 2004), 23.
5. Daisy Wademan, "The Best Advice I Ever Got," *Harvard Business Review*, January 2005, 44.
6. A. G. Lafley, "What Only the CEO Can Do," *Harvard Business Review*, May 2009, 60.
7. Margaret Stender, presentation at the Kellogg School of Management, September 15, 2012.
8. Adam Bryant, "Fix the Problem, and Not Just the Symptoms," *New York Times*, October 9, 2011, 2.
9. Noel Tichy and Ram Charan, "Speed, Simplicity, Self-Confidence: An Interview with Jack Welch," *Harvard Business Review*, September–October 1989, 4.
10. Sheena S. Iyengar and Mark R. Lepper, "When Choice Is Demotivating: Can One Desire Too Much of a Good Thing?" *Journal of Personality and Social Psychology*, December 2000.
11. Walter Isaacson, *Steve Jobs* (New York: Simon & Schuster, 2011), 343.

6 THE PLANNING PROCESS

1. James C. Collins and Jerry I. Porras, "Building Your Company's Vision," *Harvard Business Review*, September–October 1996, 65.
2. Thomas A. Stewart and Louise O'Brien, "Execution without Excuses," *Harvard Business Review*, March 2005, 109.
3. Collins and Porras, "Building Your Company's Vision," 73.
4. John J. Gabarro and John P. Kotter, "Managing Your Boss," *Harvard Business Review*, January 2005, 98.
5. Daisy Wademan, "The Best Advice I Ever Got," *Harvard Business Review*, January 2005, 44.

6. Susan Carey, "Changing the Course of JetBlue," *Wall Street Journal*, June 21, 2007, B2.
7. Kortney Stringer and Ann Zimmerman, "Polishing Penny's Image," *Wall Street Journal*, May 7, 2004, B5.
8. Andy Grove, *Only the Paranoid Survive* (New York: Crown Business, 1999), 155.

7   WRITING THE PLAN

1. Peter F. Drucker, "Managing Oneself," *Harvard Business Review*, January 2005, 103.
2. Thomas A. Stewart and Louise O'Brien, "Execution without Excuses," *Harvard Business Review*, March 2005, 108.
3. Daisy Wademan, "The Best Advice I Ever Got," *Harvard Business Review*, January 2005, 44.
4. Noel Tichy and Ram Charan, "Speed, Simplicity, Self-Confidence: An Interview with Jack Welch," *Harvard Business Review*, September–October 1989, 3.
5. Jim Kilts, *Doing What Matters: How to Get Results That Make a Difference* (New York: Crown Business, 2007), 264.

8   PRESENTING: THE BIG SHOW

1. Annie Lennox, interviewed by Alison Beard, "Life's Work," *Harvard Business Review*, October 2010, 152.
2. Bob Garfield, *And Now a Few Words from Me* (New York: McGraw-Hill, 2003), 138.
3. Herminia Ibarra and Kent Lineback, "What's Your Story?" *Harvard Business Review*, January 2005, 71.
4. Daniel Okrent, "Numbed by the Numbers, When They Just Don't Add Up," *New York Times*, January 23, 2005, sec. 4, 2.
5. Remarks of Bill Gates at Harvard University Commencement, June 7, 2007, *Harvard Gazette*, http://news.harvard.edu/gazette/story/2007/06/remarks-of-bill-gates-harvard-commencement-2007, last accessed May 21, 2012.

11   COMMON QUESTIONS

1. Julie Schlosser, "Don't Picture the Audience Naked," *Fortune*, November 25, 2002, 46.
2. James M. Kilts, *Doing What Matters: How to Get Results That Make a Difference* (New York: Crown Business, 2007), 42.

3. Alexander Chernev, *The Marketing Plan Handbook* (Chicago: Cerebellum Press, 2011), 77.

4. John A. Byrne, "The Fast Company Interview: Jeff Immelt," *Fast Company*, July 2005, 64.

5. Malcolm McDonald, *Marketing Plans*, 5th ed. (Oxford, UK: Butterworth-Heinemann), xvii.

6. Clayton M. Christensen, *The Innovator's Dilemma* (New York: HarperCollins, 2000), 225.

SOURCE NOTES

THIS BOOK IS BASED ON both research and personal experience. Over the past decade, I have talked to dozens of marketing executives about how to create a good marketing plan. I talked to people running businesses, people who have written and reviewed marketing plans. It only makes sense to build a book about marketing plans based on input from practicing executives because these are the people with the most experience in the field. Academic theory is relevant for marketing plans, of course, but a marketing plan is a tool, and the people with the keenest sense for how to create a better tool are the people who use the tool all the time.

The executives I met with worked at a wide range of organizations, including large, well-established companies and start-ups. I met with executives from industries including consumer packaged goods, health care, financial services, industrial chemicals, and technology. Many of the people I spoke with had global experience. Most of the people I interviewed were marketers by training, though almost all of them considered themselves general managers. Indeed, a good marketer is really a business leader. In my research I spoke with executives who had experience at some of the world's leading companies, including Nestlé, Unilever, Johnson & Johnson, Eli Lilly, Kodak, Pepsi, Prudential, and Pfizer. In total, the executives I interviewed had written or reviewed well over a thousand marketing plans.

This book also draws upon my own experiences creating and using marketing plans. Prior to joining the faculty at Northwestern University's Kellogg School of Management, I spent eleven years in marketing at Kraft Foods. At Kraft, each summer was marked by the annual marketing plan process. I wrote and reviewed dozens of marketing plans at Kraft, for brands including Miracle Whip, Taco Bell, DiGiorno, A.1. steak sauce, Parkay margarine, Seven Seas salad dressing, and Bull's-Eye BBQ sauce. In addition, I headed up the marketing planning process for key business units. During my time at Kraft, I wrote a few wonderful marketing plans, and I wrote a few clunkers. I learned from both. Since joining the Kellogg faculty, I have had the opportunity to work directly with many of the world's best companies, such as Eli Lilly, Pfizer, Northwestern Mutual, Microsoft, Ford, Sony, McDonald's, JPMorgan Chase, General Electric, and BP.

Finally, this book reflects my experiences at Kellogg, where I have taught some of the best and brightest marketing students in the world. For more than a decade, I have taught a course on marketing strategy. As part of the class, students participate in a business simulation, where they manage a company over the course of seven periods. Each round, the students create plans and implement programs; they can launch new products, change prices, invest in advertising, and expand or reduce their sales force. During the simulation, I have students write and present marketing plans. This has been an eye-opening experience for me. After reviewing more than a thousand of these marketing plans, I have learned that some things work and some things don't. Most importantly, I have seen firsthand that people don't naturally write great marketing plans; it is a skill that has to be learned through instruction and experience.

ACKNOWLEDGMENTS

ONE OF THE GREAT THINGS ABOUT WORKING in the world of marketing is that you have the opportunity to interact with smart, dynamic, and helpful people. Dozens of individuals contributed to this book in different ways. My only concern is that it is impossible to mention everyone who helped.

The marketing executives I interviewed, many of whom are named and quoted in the text, shared experiences and best practices. In many ways, their insights are the heart of the book. I am much in their debt. In particular, Roland Jacobs and Stuart Baum read early drafts and provided constructive feedback on the first edition. Greg Wozniak shared his insights and helped refine my thinking in several critical areas. Mark Silveira, author of *Ordinary Advertising. And How to Avoid It Like the Plague*, encouraged me to keep the project moving and provided invaluable advice on the writing process. Dawn Pickett Leijon and Kathleen Carroll provided terrific insights and examples. The Marketing Executives Networking Group (MENG) helped me connect with many sharp and savvy marketers and provided a valuable forum for sharing ideas. I am lucky to be part of the group.

I am grateful to the leadership team at Flahavan's, John Flahavan and John Noonan, for allowing me to use their company as one of the marketing plan examples.

I am particularly in debt to my students at Northwestern University's Kellogg School of Management. For more than a decade they have challenged me, kept me on my toes, and pushed me to refine my thinking and frameworks. Ryan Farnan, Matt Fitzgerald, Matt Hanculak, Matt House, and Chris Reynolds deserve particular thanks; they wrote the Edzo's marketing plan.

The marketing faculty at the Kellogg School of Management helped enormously with this project, providing both inspiration and good ideas. Professors Greg Carpenter, Lakshman Krishnamurthi, Phil Kotler, Julie Hennessy, and Alex Chernev all made substantial contributions to the book. I had the very good fortune to work with Alice Tybout on *Kellogg on Branding*. Andrew Razeghi, Steve Rogers, and Bob Schieffer, all authors, encouraged me to pursue the project and shared insights from their experience. My administrator, Subarna Ranjit, helped me with this project from the very start. I am in debt to Deans Dipak Jain and Sally Blount for their support and leadership.

My agent, David Hale Smith, provided useful guidance and helped make this book a reality. The team at Palgrave Macmillan has been supportive from the start of the project. Laurie Harting in particular encouraged me to complete this second edition.

I am particularly thankful to Patty Dowd Schmitz, who worked closely with me on the first edition of this book. Her candid feedback was both motivating and helpful. Hilary Richardson provided valuable input on this second edition.

Finally, I am in debt to my family, Carol, Claire, Charlie, and Anna, for making me laugh and reminding me that the key to a full life is balance.

INDEX